Practical Life Skills for Young Adults

Master Adulting 101 With Simple Strategies for Financial Literacy, Home Maintenance, and Smart Cooking to Build Lasting Confidence and Independence

Noah Clark

Copyright Page

Published by
Sprague Brook Publishing LLC
Paperback ISBN: 979-8-9947643-0-5
Printed in the United States of America

Legal Notice

Disclaimer

Contents

Introduction

Let me take you back to the night I officially realized I had no idea how to be an adult. It was close to 10 p.m., and I was standing in my kitchen, stomach growling, locked in a stare down with a pot of what was *supposed* to be mac and cheese. I swear I followed the instructions, but somehow the noodles had morphed into one giant, gluey blob, and the cheese sauce looked like it came straight out of a sci-fi horror movie. Let's just say it was more "science experiment gone wrong" than "comfort food." Then, because things weren't dramatic enough, the smoke alarm started blaring to announce my failure to the entire building. As I waved a towel like a maniac trying to shut it up, I remember thinking, *Wait... is this adulthood?* Okay, maybe it wasn't quite that bad, but you get the idea.

And that was just the beginning. I've overstuffed the washing machine, creating a nice pool on the floor; locked myself out of my apartment; and called my mom more times than I can count, asking things like "what does 'simmer' mean?" or "I shrank my favorite sweater—can I *unshrink* it somehow?" If you've ever found yourself struggling to fold a fitted sheet or nodding like you understand how taxes work when you have no clue, welcome. You're not alone. You're the newest member of the club.

Let's be honest—adulting is messy and weird. One day, you're feeling like a rockstar because you remembered to fill the gas tank before it ran empty, and the next, you're staring at a health insurance form, wondering if moving back home is a reasonable option. Nobody hands you a rulebook when you turn 18. School might have taught you about the Magna Carta, but no one taught you how to budget, deal with roommate drama, or clean out a clogged drain. So, if you're feeling overwhelmed, confused, or just plain frustrated that you were never taught any of this, step back and take a breath. You're not broken. You're just figuring it out, like the rest of us.

That's exactly why I wrote this book. *Practical Life Skills for Young Adults* is your starter kit for real-world confidence. No lecture halls. No boring jargon. Just real talk and step-by-step strategies that actually work. This book is here to help you figure out the basics, dodge common screw-ups, and maybe even laugh while you do it.

Here's how it works: Each chapter tackles a life skill you actually need. We'll cover things like how to handle your money without wanting to cry, how to cook food you'll want to eat, and how to fix stuff in your home without calling your parents every five minutes. Every chapter gives you easy instructions, checklists you can use, real-life examples, and a quiz at the end (with answers, because nobody needs more surprises in their life).

You're probably wondering, *Who is this person telling me how to adult?* Fair question. I'm someone who survived moving out, learned to budget when my bank account was lower than my phone battery, and figured out how to cook meals that didn't come from a box. I've dealt with weird roommates, leaky roofs, job interviews that went sideways, and grocery shopping on a shoestring. I didn't grow up with a silver spoon or a YouTube channel full of life hacks. I learned things the hard way, so you don't have to.

So, what are we going to cover? A little bit of everything you need to start running your life:

- **Money stuff:** Budgeting, saving, paying bills, and not getting scammed, so you can sleep at night instead of panicking about your bank balance
- **Home basics:** Cleaning, laundry, minor repairs, and keeping your space from turning into a health hazard
- **Cooking that doesn't suck:** Real meals, not just cereal and microwave noodles; plus, how to grocery shop without blowing your budget
- **Finding and keeping a job:** From résumés to interviews to what to do when your boss is a total whack job
- **Time management and getting stuff done:** So your to-do list stops haunting your dreams
- **Emotional intelligence:** Handling stress, relationships, and all those feelings that pop up when you least expect them
- **Digital life:** Online safety, digital etiquette, and keeping your information out of the wrong hands

This isn't just another book to read once and forget. It's designed so you can flip to the part you need when you need it. Can't remember how often to change your sheets? Check the list. Need to know what to bring to a job interview? There's a checklist for that. Curious about what makes up your credit score? Check the chart.

Every chapter comes packed with practical tools. You'll find lists for your daily, weekly, and annual chores. There's a rundown of documents you need to keep handy (and where to put them so you can find them again). You'll see troubleshooting tips for when things go sideways. And yes, there are quizzes at the end of each chapter, complete with answers, so you can check your progress (or just challenge your friends and see who's the bigger adult).

Think of this book as your personal cheat sheet for life. If you run into a mess you don't know how to clean up, this book is for you. If you need to fix something, cook something, or just not screw up your taxes, flip to the page and get going. You don't have to know everything right now. Nobody does. The trick is having a place to turn when life throws a curveball.

So, are you ready to begin? You don't have to figure this all out today. You just have to start somewhere, and this book is your somewhere. Keep it close. Take notes. Dog-ear the pages. Come back whenever you need a nudge, a laugh, or a little guidance. Because adulting isn't a finish line; it's a journey. And you? You're going to crush it.

Let's get started.

Chapter 1

Adulting Mindset and Self-Confidence

H ere's a confession: The first time I tried to buy toilet paper on my own, I lingered in the aisle for 15 minutes, overwhelmed by choices such as "triple-ply," "mega roll," and "aloe-infused." No one warns you about these moments. You think that if you survived calculus, shopping should be easy, but suddenly, you're texting your roommate for advice while blocking an older woman's cart. This is what growing up often looks like—faking confidence, second-guessing yourself, and hoping you don't leave the store with paper towels by mistake.

Demystifying Adulting—What It Really Means

Let's be real about "adulting," a word you hear everywhere, from social media to your friends joking after doing their laundry. For previous generations, *adulthood* meant significant milestones, such as marriage, owning a house, securing a steady job, or perhaps getting a family dog. It was about reaching certain markers. Today, adulting is less about those big events and more about navigating a constant stream of everyday responsibilities. It's remembering to schedule your own dentist appointments, troubleshooting your Wi-Fi, or learning to cook something other than instant ramen.

The reality is that adulting means you're learning how to adapt to whatever life throws at you. One day, you might pay your first utility bill; the next, you could lose your wallet. Perhaps your only motivation for cleaning the microwave is the bad smell. These moments aren't glamorous, but they're as real as adult life gets. Modern adulthood blends independence, creative problem-solving, and a readiness to tackle issues, even if it means calling customer service and getting stuck in endless automated menus.

Many people wrongly assume adulting means having all the answers, but the truth is that nobody does. "Fake adult" anxiety is common, especially when everyone online seems to have it together, showing off "#blessed" brunches and tidy spaces. Social media is only the highlight reel. It hides the burnt pancakes and the dirty dishes just outside the shot. Everyone feels lost sometimes, wondering if they're the only one Googling how to boil an egg (you're not). Behind those filtered photos, most people are figuring it out as they go along. You just can't see it.

Another myth is that some are just "naturally" good at adulting. Not true. No one wakes up fully equipped with every adult skill. Adulting is a mix of small abilities you pick up by making mistakes and learning as you go. You don't need an instruction manual—just curiosity and a willingness to try. The perfect adult doesn't exist. Even your mom has gotten confused by insurance paperwork or shrunk her favorite sweater in the wash.

Take my friend Jennifer. She moved into her first apartment and didn't realize she had to set up her own utilities. She spent the night in the dark, eating takeout by flashlight because she thought the power would work automatically. Or Mark, who lost his wallet before a job interview and had to replace his ID with a vague sense of where the DMV was. They both managed to get through it and now easily handle such challenges. These aren't failures but important learning moments. They are part of everyone's journey to handling life on their own.

Quick Reflection: Real Adulting Moments

Think back: What was your first "adulting" experience? Perhaps it was making your own appointment, discussing rent with your landlord, or fixing the Wi-Fi just before a big deadline. Jot it down. It's a reminder that these moments are normal, and each one helps you build new skills for next time.

Tackling Imposter Syndrome and Building Self-Esteem

Imposter syndrome has this sneaky way of making you feel like you're faking adulthood, even when you're doing everything right. Picture this: You land your first real job, manage to figure out the coffee maker in the break room, and even dress like you sort of know what "business casual" means. But inside, there's this gnawing suspicion that, at any moment, someone will walk in, point at you, and declare, "You don't belong here!" That's imposter syndrome in action, when you feel like a fraud despite your achievements. It's especially common when everything around you is new—a new apartment, a new job, or new routines. The symptoms? Second-guessing every decision, worrying about being "found out," and secretly assuming everyone else has a secret adult manual you never received. Comparing yourself to friends or siblings doesn't help. You might see what looks like flawless confidence from them, but meanwhile, you're over here Googling "how to unclog a drain" for the fourth time this month.

This self-doubt is more common than most people admit. In fact, it's often a sign that you're stepping outside your comfort zone and growing into new roles. Feeling unsure means you care about doing things right, but the trick is not letting that doubt run the show. Instead of letting it spiral, try reframing those thoughts: *I don't know everything... yet.* Treat self-doubt as a nudge, a reminder that you're learning, not proof you're failing. Everyone who's ever started something new has felt like an imposter at some point. That includes the person who invented the phrase "Fake it till you make it." (Honestly, that entire saying is based on the universal experience of winging it.)

Developing Confidence

One practical way to boost your confidence is to keep a "wins journal." It's as simple as it sounds: Get a notebook or open a note on your phone and jot down any little victory at the end of each day. Made your own lunch instead of ordering out? Write it down. Sent an email to your landlord without having a panic attack? That's a win. Did you pay a bill before the final notice arrived? Victory! Over time, these small achievements stack up and remind you that you're doing more than you realize.

Another strategy is breaking big challenges into micro-goals. Instead of "become a financial genius," start with "track my spending for one week." Celebrate every milestone, no matter how minor it may seem. Confidence isn't something you're born with; it develops through repetition and exposure to new situations. The more times you take action—no matter how awkwardly—the less intimidating it becomes.

The myth that confidence is some magical trait certain people "have" is one of adulthood's greatest scams. Even celebrities have shared stories about feeling insecure at the start of their careers. Lady Gaga admitted she felt like an outsider early on; Tom Hanks has openly discussed his struggles with self-doubt, even after winning awards. What separates them from everyone else isn't natural-born swagger; it's the willingness to show up again and again and learn on the fly.

If self-talk is running wild with negativity, try flipping the script. Instead of thinking, *I'm so bad at this*, try, *I'm still learning, and that's okay*. If all else fails, find one thing you did well today, even if it's just remembering to take out the trash or waking up before noon. Nobody expects you to have everything together. Turns out, nobody else does, either.

Interactive Exercise: Your Wins Journal

Grab a piece of paper or open your favorite notes app. At the end of each day this week, jot down one thing— big or small—that made you feel even slightly accomplished. Did you finally sort your laundry by color? Did you ask a question in class or at work? Each little win adds up to proof that adulting doesn't require perfection so much as progress and persistence.

Growth Mindset vs. Perfectionism—How to Embrace Mistakes

Perfectionism is the sneaky villain in the story of adulting. It whispers that you need a flawless résumé before applying for a job, a spotless kitchen before inviting friends over, or a perfect plan before trying anything new. It's that voice saying, "Don't even bother unless you're sure you won't mess up." The result? You freeze. You stare at a job listing for days because your résumé has a typo you just cannot find. Or you skip trying a new recipe because what if you burn

15

dinner...again? This is perfectionist paralysis, and it's the single biggest roadblock to learning anything new as an adult. You get stuck in a loop of overthinking, convinced that mistakes are proof you're not cut out for this grown-up stuff.

Now, let's contrast that with a growth mindset, which can be a game-changer. A growth mindset is about believing that skills aren't fixed; you can improve and get better with effort and practice. Instead of fearing mistakes, you start to see them as stepping stones, not brick walls. You shift from *I failed, so I'm hopeless* to *I failed, so I learned something*. Suddenly, burning dinner isn't a disaster; it's a lesson in why smoke detectors exist. Over-drafting your bank account doesn't mean you're doomed with money; it means you now know how to set up balance alerts and triple-check your account before swiping your card at Taco Tuesday.

Mistakes are like the tuition for adulthood—no one escapes paying. For example, I once paid my rent late because I relied on memory instead of setting a calendar reminder. Cue the late fee and a stern email from the landlord. Embarrassing? Yes. Did I ever pay late again? Nope. That sting became the lesson that taught me to organize my bills better. The next time something goes sideways, try asking yourself, *What did I learn?* This simple question stops negative self-talk in its tracks and turns a facepalm moment into a building block.

Positive Self-Talk

Reframing the way you talk to yourself is key. Instead of *I can't do this*, tack on a *yet*. Suddenly, *I can't cook anything except toast* becomes *I can't cook anything except toast...yet*. That tiny word flips the script and opens the door to improvement. Want some growth-mindset affirmations? Try these: *Every mistake is proof I'm trying, Progress beats perfection*, and *Skills are built, not born*.

Setting realistic goals helps, too. Ditch the idea of becoming an overnight expert. Start with something you can actually finish, like learning how to cook three meals you won't mind eating all week or creating a simple budget that tracks your money without needing a spreadsheet PhD. These are SMART goals: Specific, Measurable, Achievable, Relevant, and Time-bound. For example, "I'll cook one homemade dinner (specific, measurable) each week (achievable) for a month (time-bound)" is way less intimidating than "I'll become a chef by Friday."

When things go sideways (they will), use self-compassion statements to cut yourself some slack: *Everyone burns dinner at some point* or *Nobody gets everything right on the first try*. These reminders aren't cheesy; they're necessary repairs to all the damage perfectionism can do.

If you need proof that failing forward works, look at anyone who has become proficient at something adults do every day. My friend Sarah applied for 20 jobs before she landed her first genuine offer. Each rejection taught her how to tweak her cover letter and interview answers until she finally got a yes. Another friend once over-drafted his account by buying late-night pizzas, and now he has alerts set up so he never dips below zero again. These common stories are proof that mistakes teach more than safe choices ever could.

Growth-Mindset Exercise: "What Did I Learn?" Journaling

Tonight, write down one thing that didn't go as planned this week. Underneath it, list out what you learned, what you'll do differently next time, and one thing you did right, even if it's just trying in the first place. Keep this habit going for a month, and see how much more confident you feel about handling curveballs.

Creating Your Personal Independence Plan

Independence doesn't pop out of thin air. You don't wake up one morning magically able to keep plants alive, sort your mail, and whip up a risotto while your laundry spins quietly in the background. It takes intention, and sometimes, a little tough love in the form of a self-assessment. Think of it as a personal inventory—not to shame yourself, but to see where you stand. Grab a pen, open your notes app, or talk to yourself in the mirror, or do whatever works for you. Create a checklist of life tasks you can do without help, and identify areas where you still feel uncertain. Can you run a washing machine without flooding the laundry room? Do you know how to check your bank balance and read a pay stub? Ever cooked a meal that didn't involve boiling water and a flavor packet? List out basics like doing laundry (including not mixing reds with whites), preparing simple meals, following a budget, making appointments, keeping your space clean, and handling minor emergencies (like what to do when you lock yourself out). Be honest. Nobody's grading this.

Now, let's get personal: What does independence actually mean for you? Forget what Instagram or your second cousin says. Maybe it's moving out on your own or just learning how to cook dinner three nights in a row. Think about where you want more freedom or confidence. Is it managing your money, keeping your home in order, or building better routines? Ask yourself: *When do I feel most self-reliant? When do I feel stuck?* Write down the situations in which being more independent would make life smoother or less stressful. Maybe you want to stop panicking when the Wi-Fi goes down, or perhaps you dream of feeling calm when it's time to pay bills. Your independence plan should reflect your reality, not someone else's highlight reel.

Breaking Down Goals

Big goals are nice in theory, but they can freeze you faster than an unexpected bill. Break them down into micro-actions. If your dream is to move into your own place, don't start by browsing luxury apartments on Zillow. First step: Check your monthly income and expenses. Next, research what rent costs in different neighborhoods. After that, set up an automatic savings transfer each month for your deposit fund. Then, make an apartment viewing checklist considering items such as smoke alarms, water pressure, and any unusual smells. If cooking feels like an Olympic event, start by picking one recipe and making a shopping list for it. Go to the store and buy those ingredients—no substitutions for now. Follow the recipe step-by-step. If it's edible and half the smoke detector batteries are still working at the end, that's progress.

To keep from backsliding into old habits or losing motivation after week two, you need regular check-ins with yourself. Set calendar reminders—weekly for small habits, monthly for bigger goals. Use apps or even sticky notes on the fridge if tech isn't your thing. Review what worked, what fizzled out, and what needs tweaking. Nobody gets every step right the first time. If you fall off track (like realizing you haven't cooked in two weeks), don't spiral out of control. Adjust your plan: Maybe batch-cooking on Sundays fits better than nightly dinners. If budgeting is falling flat because tracking every penny feels like torture, consider switching to a simpler system—perhaps just tallying your food expenses for one week.

Life Skills Independence Checklist

- **Budgeting (knowing monthly incomes/expenses)**
- **Cleaning (kitchen, bathroom, floors)**
- **Cooking three basic meals**
- **Grocery shopping with a list**
- **Handling minor emergencies (locked out, lost keys)**
- **Laundry (sorting colors, choosing cycles)**
- **Making appointments (doctor/dentist)**
- **Paying bills on time**
- **Reading a pay stub**
- **Setting up bank alerts**

Review this list every month. Highlight skills you've nailed and pick one to focus on next. Independence is like leveling up in a game where the challenges keep changing. The trick is to keep playing and tweaking your strategy as you go.

Building a Support Squad for Accountability and Encouragement

Trying to build new life skills solo is like trying to assemble IKEA furniture without instructions (or an Allen wrench). Sure, you could do it, but you're going to shed unnecessary sweat, mutter a few choice words, and maybe end up with a bookshelf that's more "abstract sculpture" than storage. That's where your support squad comes in. Having a crew—friends, mentors, even a few wise internet strangers —doesn't just make things easier; it supercharges your growth and makes the whole process a lot less lonely. You'll find that people pushing one another forward makes everyone braver and more likely to stick with new habits. Imagine trying to learn how to meal prep for the week: Alone, you might order takeout after burning your first attempt, but when your friend texts photos of their grilled chicken (which looks suspiciously like it survived a small fire), swapping tips and laughing about your mutual kitchen disasters suddenly feels less intimidating and a lot more fun.

There is a huge difference between supportive and toxic relationships. Supportive people cheer for your weird attempts at adulting, remind you it's normal to mess up, and offer honest advice instead of eye rolls. These are the ones who answer your late-night panic texts about whether you can use dish soap in the dishwasher (spoiler: don't). On the flip side, toxic connections might mock your mistakes, compete instead of collaborate, or make you feel like you're always lagging behind. It's important to recognize who brings out your resilience versus who drains your energy or confidence. A good squad makes you feel lighter, not weighed down.

It's normal to be nervous when you need to ask for help or advice. You don't want to seem needy or clueless, but the truth is that most people love being asked for their opinion. It makes them feel useful. Keep it simple and direct. If you're texting a friend or mentor for guidance, try: "Hey! I'm trying to figure out how to budget for groceries this month, and I know you've got this down. Would you mind sharing what works for you?" Or email a professor: "Hi Professor Smith, I'm interested in learning more about time management in college. If you have any tips or resources, I'd really appreciate it." There's no shame in reaching out. The only mistake is sitting in silence while Google feeds you multiple conflicting answers.

Building a Network With Variety

Don't limit your squad to people just like you. Build a network with variety—friends from different backgrounds, older adults who've made it through the rough patches, maybe even that neighbor who seems to know everyone's business (they're a goldmine for local resources). Join campus clubs, hobby groups, or online forums dedicated to life skills or your interests. You'll be surprised at how much wisdom lives in Reddit threads or Discord servers when you ask the right questions. Local meetups and community events can connect you with mentors who have weathered every storm imaginable.

Systems for accountability take peer support from a "nice idea" to real results. Find an accountability buddy, someone who will check in on your progress without letting you off the hook. Schedule a weekly call or group chat in which everyone shares what they tackled that week, big or small. You could even start a monthly "progress party," where your group celebrates wins and brainstorms solutions for whatever tripped someone up. Try group challenges like "No Takeout Week" or "Clean One Room a Day." The collective energy makes even dull chores exciting.

When you have people rooting for you, setbacks sting less, and wins feel bigger. Growth involves letting others lift you up and sharing what you learn along the way. So keep your squad close—text them when you succeed, call them when you need a pep talk, and make space for new connections whenever possible. With the right support network, every step forward is lighter and far more rewarding. Keep building those bridges. You never know when one will help you cross an unexpected river.

Quiz:

1) What is a common misconception about adulting mentioned in the chapter?

    A. It's mostly about getting married and buying a house
    B. It requires a college degree
    C. Only older adults have to do it
    D. It comes naturally to people who are responsible

Answer: A

The chapter explains that adulting today is more about handling everyday responsibilities (like setting appointments or cooking), not just hitting big life milestones like marriage or homeownership.

* * *

2) What does the author suggest as a helpful tool to boost self-confidence?

    A. Making a to-do list every morning
    B. Repeating motivational quotes out loud
    C. Keeping a "wins journal" to track small achievements
    D. Avoiding complex tasks until you feel confident

Answer: C

A "wins journal" is recommended as a way to recognize and celebrate daily victories—no matter how small—to build self-esteem and a growth mindset.

* * *

3) What is **imposter syndrome**, as described in the chapter?

A. Pretending to be someone you're not to impress others
B. Feeling like a fraud despite achieving something
C. Lying about your age or experience
D. Copying other adults' habits to fit in

Answer: B

Imposter syndrome is the feeling that you're not truly qualified or capable, even when you're succeeding. The chapter normalizes this feeling and encourages reframing it as part of growth.

* * *

4) What is the key difference between a **perfectionist mindset** and a **growth mindset?**

A. Perfectionists work harder than growth thinkers
B. Growth mindset people avoid failure
C. Perfectionists fear mistakes; growth thinkers learn from them
D. A growth mindset requires natural talent

Answer: C

A perfectionist fears messing up and often avoids trying. A growth mindset sees mistakes as learning opportunities and embraces progress over perfection.

* * *

5) Why is building a support squad important, according to the chapter?

   A. So you can borrow their stuff when yours breaks
   B. So you don't have to do chores alone
   C. Because a strong network encourages growth and accountability
   D. Because adulting is only possible in groups

Answer: C

The chapter emphasizes that having supportive friends, mentors, or communities helps you stick to goals, share knowledge, and make adulting less lonely and overwhelming.

* * *

Chapter 2

Time Management and Organization Mastery

Beyond the To-Do List—Designing a Personalized Routine

E ver stared at a to-do list so long you start wondering if the paper is judging you? You write down "clean room, answer emails, become a millionaire, figure out taxes" and instantly feel overwhelmed. The problem with classic to-do lists is that they're often just wish lists fueled by caffeine and panic. They don't account for your life or your energy, for who you really are. You end up with 20 unchecked boxes and a creeping sense of doom, which is not the vibe you're going for. Most people try to tackle everything at once, following some myth that real adults can "do it all." Reality check: Nobody gets everything done every day, and pretending otherwise is a recipe for burnout or, worse, existential dread at 3 a.m.

The secret sauce is designing routines that work for you, not some influencer who wakes up at 4:30 a.m. to meditate with their cat. Ignore the myth that you should squeeze every productive second from your day. Instead, focus on mapping when you have the most energy. Are you a morning person who wakes up ready to take on the world before breakfast? Or do you hit your stride after everyone else has gone to bed, working best in the peace and glow of midnight? If you're alert and productive in the morning, schedule heavy lifting—think studying for finals or deep work—before lunch. Save lighter tasks, such as emails or folding laundry, for the afternoon. If you're a night owl, flip it. Do routine stuff early and save your creative or brain-intensive work for when you're buzzing later on.

Keeping Track of Your Energy

Building a custom routine starts by tracking your energy highs and lows for a week. Grab a notebook (or use your Notes app) and jot down when you feel laser-focused versus when your brain turns to soup. Once you spot patterns, structure your days around them. For college students, mornings may be spent on classes or review sessions, afternoons on group meetings, and evenings catching up on assignments or decompressing. If you're working an entry-level job, block out time before your shift for errands or self-care, use breaks wisely (stretch, hydrate, doomscroll responsibly), and plan downtime after work to avoid zombie mode. Freelancers or gig workers might find their schedules are less predictable, so batch similar tasks on flexible days and build in buffer time for last-minute gigs.

Interactive Exercise: Build Your Real-Life Routine

1. **Write down everything you do on a "typical" day (don't worry; nobody's routine is glamorous —if "scroll TikTok" is on there, you're normal).**
2. **Circle the stuff that absolutely *must* happen (class at 9 a.m., work shift, picking up meds).**
3. **Note when you feel awake versus when you want to nap under your desk.**
4. **Slot the non-negotiables into your best energy windows.**
5. **Fill in the rest: meals, laundry, fun activities, even doomscroll time (in moderation!).**

6. **Try it for a week, then review. What felt good? What was chaos? Adjust as needed.**

The key to success is regular self-check-ins. Every month (or, honestly, whenever life gets weird), look at what's working and what's not. Maybe your job hours change or classes swap days. Routines should flex with you—rigidity is for robots and oatmeal cookies. Ask yourself: *Am I always tired at the end of the day? Are important things slipping through the cracks? Do I have any fun anymore?* If these are the case, tweak your routine until it fits again, because life isn't static, and neither are you.

Time-Blocking Hacks for Work, Study, and Life

Time-blocking is like giving your day a playlist—each part gets its own track, and you decide when to hit play. Instead of letting your to-do list run wild, you chunk your time into blocks and give each block a job. Maybe it's "study for chem," "work on résumé," or "finally tackle the laundry monster." When you group similar tasks together, you focus better and cut down on that weird, exhausting feeling when you bounce from math homework to texting friends to remembering you need to defrost the chicken. Multitasking drains your brain way faster than actually getting stuff done one at a time. Time-blocking helps you avoid that, so you spend less time spinning your wheels and more time actually finishing things.

Color-coding your blocks takes this up a notch. Picture your week as a rainbow—blue for classes, green for work shifts, yellow for chores, purple for downtime. Grab some highlighters or use the color options in Google Calendar, then assign a color to each category of life. Soon, your planner (or phone) will look like a unicorn exploded, but you'll instantly see where your energy is going. For example, if Thursday is 80% blue (study), it might be time to add a green (gym) or purple (friend hangout) block to keep things balanced. If you're more visual, drawing your schedule out on paper or using sticky notes can make it feel less digital and more real.

To build a balanced day or week with time-blocking, start by scheduling the non-negotiables—classes, work hours, and appointments. Next, insert blocks for focused work or study, using longer chunks for more challenging tasks and shorter bursts for easier ones. Sprinkle in breaks; your brain absolutely needs them. Trust me, nobody wins productivity points for sitting in front of a screen until their eyes glaze over. Add buffer zones between activities so you're not running from one thing to the next like you're in an action movie. For instance, if you finish work at 5 p.m., don't schedule dinner with friends at 5:05. Give yourself some breathing room to transition, grab a snack, or stare at the ceiling and decompress.

If you find yourself constantly scrambling because tasks spill over or take longer than planned, use catch-up blocks. These are open spaces in your schedule where you can finish anything that ran late or deal with surprise homework from that one professor who loves pop quizzes. Over-scheduling is a classic trap; your calendar gets packed, something inevitably takes longer than expected, and suddenly, you're behind and stressed. Build in extra time for everything, and don't beat yourself up if you need to move things around on the fly.

Interruptions are another sneaky enemy. If you get derailed midblock (thanks, group chat), pause and decide: Can this interruption wait? If not, reschedule your current block or shorten it so you can handle the new task without disrupting your whole day. Flexibility is key—life isn't set in stone, and neither is your calendar.

Prioritizing Like a Pro: The Eisenhower Matrix in Real Life

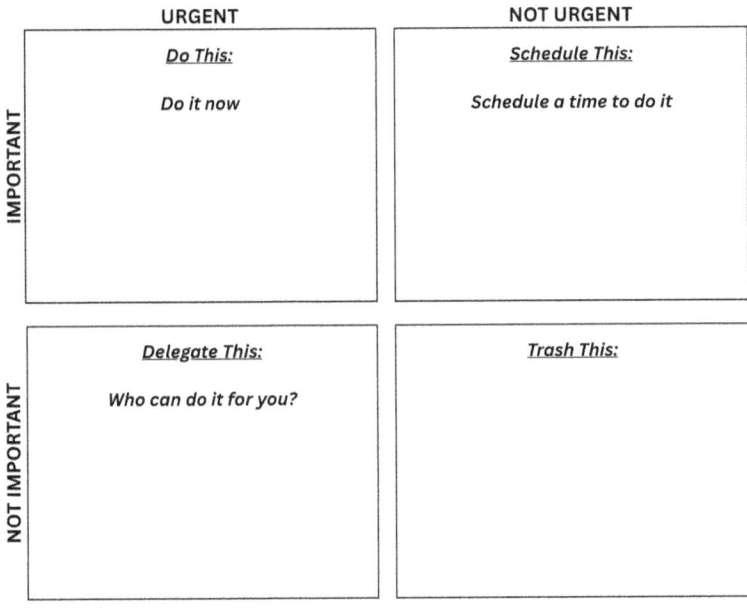

Let's be honest: Sometimes your week feels like a game of whack-a-mole, with tasks popping up everywhere and no clue which one to smack first. That's precisely where the Eisenhower Matrix comes in. Picture a box divided into four squares. On one side, you've got "urgent" and "not urgent." On the other, "important" and "not important." Suddenly, you can sort your chaos visually, and it's weirdly satisfying. Here's how the squares break down: The top-left is urgent and important (for example, your essay due at midnight or the car that needs gas before work). The top-right is important but not urgent (such as prepping for finals or refreshing your résumé). The bottom-left is urgent but not important (maybe your group chats are blowing up about dinner plans). And the bottom-right? Not urgent, not important (for example, scrolling memes or organizing your sock drawer by color).

Imagine Your Week

You've got a lab report, bills to pay, friend drama, a fridge that smells like something crawled in and died, and a birthday gift to buy. Grab a piece of paper and draw those four squares. Now, start dropping each task where it fits. Is the lab report due tomorrow? Urgent and important. Birthday shopping for your cousin next month? Important but not urgent—schedule it for later. That group chat? Urgent (they want answers), but, let's be real, not important. Memes and doomscrolling? They can wait... unless you want a PhD in procrastination.

Try this exercise at the start of your week: List every single thing on your mind—schoolwork, chores, social stuff, even calling Grandma. Put each one in the appropriate quadrant. You'll probably notice your "urgent/important" box is packed because you've been fighting fires instead of planning ahead. The trick is to start shifting more tasks to the top-right—important but not urgent—so you're working ahead instead of running on panic and caffeine.

Using the matrix regularly helps you spot patterns. Perhaps you often prioritize self-care activities (such as sleep or exercise) as "not urgent," so they never get done. That's a trap. Schedule those as if they were dinner with Beyoncé—i.e., non-negotiable. If you overload the "urgent" column, you're setting yourself up for burnout or a meltdown when everything hits at once. Notice which tasks keep landing in "urgent but not important." These are time-thieves—for example, text replies that can wait, meetings that could've been emails, or errands you do to avoid real work.

Color-coding your matrix can also be helpful: Use green for urgent and important tasks, yellow for important but non-urgent tasks, blue for distractions, and red for low-priority items. You can even use digital apps if paper isn't your thing; there are plenty out there that let you drag and drop tasks between quadrants with satisfying little clicks.

Sometimes, you'll need to flex your "no" muscle. If you find yourself constantly saying yes to last-minute requests that land squarely in the "not important" zone, practice politely declining. For example: "Hey, I'd love to help brainstorm theme ideas for Game Night, but I need to finish my presentation first." Self-reflection is helpful here: After each week, ask yourself what worked, what didn't, and which tasks truly deserved your attention. This way, you start living less like a firefighter and more like someone who has time to enjoy their coffee before it goes cold.

Mastering Digital Calendars and Reminder Apps

If you've ever missed an appointment because you scribbled it on the back of a receipt that now lives in the Bermuda Triangle of your back-pack, it's time to let your phone do the heavy lifting. Digital calendars are basically the cheat codes of adult life. Google Calendar is the MVP for most young adults—it's free, works anywhere you can find Wi-Fi, and plays nicely with both Android and iPhone. Color-code your classes, work shifts, birthdays, and even Taco Tuesday, and see your week at a glance. Apple Calendar is excellent if you're deeply entrenched in the Apple ecosystem; it syncs seamlessly across your iPhone, iPad, and Mac without drama. For those who love turning tasks into satisfying checked boxes, Todoist blends calendar views with powerful to-do lists and priorities. Google Keep is less of a calendar and more of a digital sticky note wall, perfect for bite-sized reminders such as "buy toothpaste" or "text Mom back."

Starting from scratch feels intimidating, but it's easier than trying to decipher your own handwriting. Open your calendar app—let's use Google Calendar as an example. Hit the "+" to create your first event. Enter the title ("Bio Lab 2 p.m." or "Laundry—no more excuses"). Set the date and time. Next, tap "add notification," so your phone gives you a heads-up beforehand. Now, for the magic: Turn on sync in settings so your calendar updates everywhere—your laptop, phone, even that old tablet you use for Netflix marathons. The trick is consistency; if you put something in your calendar on one device, it should show up everywhere else without playing hide-and-seek.

Now, let's level up: Recurring events are your new best friend. Instead of typing "pay rent" 12 times a year, just set it to repeat monthly and relax. You can do this for anything—weekly classes, work shifts, even remembering to water that sad-looking plant in your window. Tap "repeat" when making an event, choose the frequency (e.g., "every Monday," "first of the month"), and boom—automation activated. Want to make sure your roommate doesn't "forget" trash day again? Share your calendar with them. Most apps allow you to invite others, so everyone is notified when chores, bills, or group projects are due. No more group chat confusion or blaming each other when the fridge science experiment explodes.

Customizing Your Calendar

Notification fatigue is real. Nobody needs their phone barking every five minutes about things that aren't urgent. Start by customizing alerts so you only get pings for what truly matters. Choose different sounds for important events (like class or job interviews) and mellow tones for less critical stuff. Use snooze settings for reminders you can't handle at the exact moment—maybe you get a heads-up about laundry during class; snooze it for an hour so it pops up when you're free. If your phone starts to feel like a needy toddler demanding constant attention, use "do not disturb" modes during deep work or sleep. This way, important alerts still sneak through, but memes and random notifications stay silent until you're ready to deal with them.

Digital calendars aren't just for keeping life from falling apart; they make space for what matters and free up mental real estate for more interesting things than remembering when your next dentist appointment is. Once you get the hang of syncing, sharing, and actually checking your calendar, you'll wonder how you ever survived without it, even if you still occasionally forget where you put your keys.

Beating Procrastination With the Two-Minute Rule

Procrastination is like having a persistent, unwanted roommate in your head always trying to convince you that tomorrow is better for getting things done or that Netflix or reorganizing your sock drawer suddenly matter more than your true priorities. We've all faced it—a looming task grows more overwhelming the longer we ignore it. Usually, this happens because our brains instinctively dodge anything that seems tedious, complex, or endless. When you confront a big job—for example, "write that research paper" or "clean your closet"—your mind instantly throws up warning signals: too much effort, too daunting, not worth the trouble right now. So you avoid, distract yourself, and procrastinate until you're left scrambling at the last second.

This is where the two-minute rule steps in. The rule is simple: If something will take less than two minutes, do it right away. Don't overthink or negotiate with yourself. The power of this rule comes from bypassing inertia. Even the smallest action delivers a sense of completion, triggering a brief hit of accomplishment (thanks, dopamine). That feeling helps build momentum, making even big tasks seem more manageable. For example, consider responding to a brief email, tossing dirty socks in the hamper, or adding an appointment to your calendar—each is quicker to do than to procrastinate about it.

You can apply this to tackle bigger jobs by breaking them into bite-sized actions that take less than two minutes each. Don't tell yourself to "write a paper"—that's overwhelming. Instead, just "open the document" or "write one sentence." Once you start, it's much easier to keep going. For daunting calls, first "find the number," then "dial."

For taxes, "locate last year's folder." Breaking a task into laughably small actions is far more effective than waiting for a surge of motivation.

Try a quick exercise: List three tasks you've been putting off this week. For each one, write down the smallest possible first step that takes under two minutes. Now, do just that first step without thinking about anything beyond it. If your desk is a disaster, start by tossing one receipt. For an overflowing inbox, reply to the easiest message or archive a handful. Watch how these tiny actions start to build momentum. Soon, you'll be making real progress and wondering why you waited.

Here's a real-life example: My desk once looked like it survived a paper tornado and a snack-food explosion. Every day, I told myself I'd clean it "after just one more podcast episode," but nothing changed. When I finally applied the two-minute rule—simply tossing one empty can on day one, wiping crumbs the next, and then organizing a paper pile—I saw a dramatic improvement in just one week. The same happened with my emails: Replying to just one message each morning snowballed into tackling dozens by the end of the week. These tiny wins snowball, turning untamable messes into manageable ones.

Weekly and Monthly Reset Rituals for Staying on Track

Letting your backpack become a black hole or your workspace pile up with snack wrappers can quickly derail a productive week. Clutter and chaos build quickly when you're handling classes, work, friendships, and all the random adult responsibilities. That's why weekly and monthly reset rituals are your secret weapon for avoiding overwhelm. Think of them as regular check-ins, a chance to hit refresh before things spiral out of control. These resets help you focus on what matters, catch up on what's falling behind, and keep your goals visible instead of buried under random receipts and a half-finished to-do list. When these routines become a habit, staying organized feels less overwhelming and more manageable.

Start your weekly reset by tackling your bag or workspace. Clear out old receipts, wrappers, and any other items you no longer need. Wipe down surfaces, untangle chargers, and discard expired or unused items. Review last week's unfinished tasks—don't just move them over blindly. Decide whether they're still important or whether you can let them go. This is also a good time to plan your meals (even if it's just picking cereal nights), organize errands, and confirm upcoming appointments or deadlines. The goal isn't a perfect, Instagram-ready desk; rather, you're clearing mental space so you can focus on what's actually important.

Once a month, dive a little deeper. Pull out your calendar or notes app and reflect for a few minutes on what went well and what tripped you up. Did you hit a big goal or get through a tough week? Jot it down. Simple prompts, such as "What did I accomplish?" or "What challenged me?" can provide clarity. Use this time to review and adjust your bigger routines or goals as needed. If meal planning didn't work but tracking spending did, that's useful information to tweak your habits for next month.

Resets shouldn't feel like punishment. Make them enjoyable; put on a favorite playlist while you sort laundry, treat yourself to a snack afterward, or team up for a "reset party" with a friend or roommate. If you enjoy working alone, set a timer and challenge yourself to see how much you can accomplish in 20 minutes; racing against the clock can be a great motivator.

Reset rituals are designed to help you keep chaos in check and make sure the important stuff doesn't slip through the cracks. These routines create breathing room and help you stay focused so you can enjoy life's good moments, like finding your headphones or remembering an assignment on time.

With these habits, staying on track becomes easier each week. You start feeling more in control, responding to life instead of just reacting. Up next, we'll tackle money matters and show you that financial independence isn't just for spreadsheet wizards or lottery winners.

Quiz:

1) What is one reason classic to-do lists often fail, according to the chapter?

    A. They're too long to read
    B. They focus only on work tasks
    C. They don't align with your real energy or schedule
    D. They are too expensive to make

Answer: C

The chapter explains that traditional to-do lists become overwhelming because they don't consider your actual time or energy levels, making them more like wish lists than realistic plans.

                                       * * *

2) What is a benefit of using time-blocking?

    A. It helps you multitask more efficiently
    B. It allows you to group similar tasks for better focus
    C. It eliminates the need for breaks
    D. It makes your schedule completely inflexible

Answer: B

Time-blocking helps you stay focused by grouping similar tasks together, reducing the brain drain caused by constantly switching contexts.

3) Which quadrant of the Eisenhower Matrix should contain tasks like "scrolling memes" or "alphabetizing your sock drawer"?

  A. Urgent and Important
  B. Important but Not Urgent
  C. Urgent but Not Important
  D. Not Urgent and Not Important

Answer: D

These are classic "Not Urgent and Not Important" tasks—things that often serve as distractions and can usually be deleted or deprioritized.

4) What is the 2-Minute Rule designed to combat?

  A. Time-zone confusion
  B. Multitasking
  C. Overplanning
  D. Procrastination

Answer: D

The 2-Minute Rule helps you beat procrastination by encouraging you to immediately handle any task that takes less than two minutes, breaking inertia and building momentum.

* * *

5) Why are weekly and monthly reset rituals recommended?

    A. To completely reorganize your room
    B. To punish yourself for falling behind
    C. To maintain control, clear clutter, and review progress
    D. To avoid using calendars and reminders

Answer: C

Reset rituals help you stay organized by clearing out physical and mental clutter, checking in on goals, and making adjustments before things spiral out of control.

* * *

Chapter 3

Financial Adulting—
Money Made Simple

Setting Up Your First Budget—A Zero-Stress Guide

Ever checked your bank app only to wonder where all your money went? Maybe it disappeared on pizza or forgotten subscriptions quietly eating away at your balance. This is where budgeting comes into play. With budgeting, you learn how to assign every dollar a job so your money works for you, not the other way around. By budgeting, you're creating options and reducing financial stress between paydays.

First, budgeting is not simply passively tracking where your money vanished to. Tracking tells you after the fact that you spent $50 on coffee, whereas *budgeting* means you've decided ahead of time how much to allocate for coffee. I'm not suggesting that you count every penny obsessively so much as I'm suggesting that you learn how to instruct your dollars to cover what matters most to you (rent, food, streaming, or whatever your priorities might be).

The 50/30/20 Method

A fundamental approach to begin mastering your finances is through the 50/30/20 budgeting principle. This method entails allocating 50% of your net income to essential expenses, such as housing, groceries, and basic utilities; 30% toward discretionary spending, including entertainment and dining out; and the remaining 20% toward savings or paying off debts. If your monthly take-home pay is $1,800, you would distribute $900 for necessities, $540 for personal indulgences, and $360 toward building your financial future or reducing financial burdens. To effectively implement this strategy, consider utilizing visual aids. Pie charts, for instance, offer a clear and immediate representation of how your income is divided among these categories, offering you a better understanding and management of your finances. Additionally, budget worksheets can serve as a practical tool, guiding you through the process of categorizing your expenses and ensuring adherence to your budgeting goals. These resources not only simplify the budgeting process but also teach you how to make informed decisions about your spending and saving habits.

The Zero-Based Method

Zero-based budgeting stands as a pivotal strategy for mastering your finances, essentially ensuring every dollar you earn has a purpose or "job" before the next paycheck arrives. Start by jotting down your total income at the top of a page. Beneath that, begin deducting your expenses, listing everything from fixed costs, such as rent, utilities, and loan payments, to variable expenses, including groceries, transportation, subscriptions, entertainment, and even occasional indulgences like snacks. The goal is to allocate your funds so meticulously that your income minus your expenditures equals zero. This method not only teaches you a disciplined approach to managing your money but also gives you the flexibility to handle unforeseen expenses—be it emergency car repairs or last-minute invitations to social gatherings—without disrupting your financial equilibrium.

Pay Yourself First Method

Adopting the "pay yourself first" strategy is a powerful tool in building financial independence. This method involves prioritizing your savings by transferring a predetermined amount into your savings account immediately after receiving your paycheck before allocating funds to other expenses. Think of this savings contribution as a non-negotiable bill, similar to rent or utilities, that you must pay each pay period. The key here is consistency over perfection; even if you can only afford to set aside a modest sum, such as $10, the act of regularly saving will accumulate over time and instill disciplined financial habits that can benefit you throughout life.

To create your starting budget:

- Gather your pay stubs, receipts, and recent bills (even those little Venmo pizza requests or random app charges).
- List every source of income: jobs, side gigs, gifts.
- Group expenses into "needs" (rent, groceries, transportation, phone) and "wants" (subscriptions, entertainment, eating out).
- If you can live without something for a month, it's likely a "want."

If your income isn't consistent—say you freelance or work gigs—use the lowest month as your planning guide. Build a buffer for slow periods or unexpected expenses, and set aside a small emergency fund in your budget to help with surprises like healthcare bills or broken headphones.

Budgeting Practice: Create Your First Monthly Budget

- **List all income sources.**
- **Write down fixed "needs": rent, groceries, transportation, phone, etc.**

- **Add up "wants": subscriptions, entertainment, takeout, etc.**
- **Set a savings goal, even if small.**
- **Subtract expenses from income until you hit zero—cut "wants" first if needed.**
- **Adjust categories as your situation changes.**

Budgeting is flexible; feel free to tweak categories or methods as your needs evolve. You want to be consistent and stay aware of where your money is flowing.

There is a link at the back of the book to download some sample budget spreadsheets.

Tracking Expenses Without Losing Your Mind (or Your Receipts)

You know that feeling when payday hits, and you swear you'll be responsible, but by the weekend, your money has Houdini'd out of your account? Expense tracking is how you stop those disappearing acts. The trick is keeping it simple enough that you'll actually do it. Some people swear by daily tracking, jotting down every swipe and Venmo transaction as if they're training for the Olympics of budgeting. Others prefer a weekly rundown, collecting all their spending and tallying it up once, maybe with a snack in hand for moral support. Daily tracking keeps you hyper-aware but can be a bit much —you don't want to become the person who won't buy gum without writing it down. Weekly check-ins are more chill, but you risk forgetting that $12 impulse latte. Find your groove; if you lose steam with daily logs, try batching it for the weekend.

Modern bank and credit card apps can do much of the heavy lifting for you. Most people automatically categorize purchases such as food, bills, shopping, and ride shares. If you use mostly cards, you can scroll through recent transactions at any time. Set up notifications or low-balance alerts so nothing sneaks past you. For cash spenders, life's trickier. The "photo your receipts" move works wonders: Snap a quick pic of every receipt on your phone before it disappears into the mysterious void of pockets and junk drawers. At the end of the week, go through your photos, sort them into albums—food, rides, random Target hauls—and marvel at your spending patterns. If you're more old school or want to curb spending, try the envelope method: Stash cash for specific categories in labeled envelopes (e.g., "Groceries," "Fun," "Coffee"), and when those envelopes are empty, that's it for the month. No more accidental $40 "just one thing" Target runs.

Regularly Reviewing Your Expenses

Reviewing where your money actually went can feel like scrolling through awkward old Facebook photos—potentially embarrassing but necessary. Once a month, sit down with your bank app, phone album, or physical receipts and color-code categories: green for groceries, blue for bills, and red for regretted purchases (looking at you, late-night Uber Eats). Use a checklist: Rent paid? Groceries on target? Did that random subscription renew again? Seeing everything color-coded makes leaks obvious. In fact, one month, I realized I'd spent more on takeout than on groceries and almost fainted (but hey, self-awareness is progress).

The wild thing about tracking is how sneaky habits change over time. Those tiny moments when you consider buying a snack or another streaming service add up fast. After one full month of consistent tracking, celebrate! Micro-milestones matter: Buy yourself a fancy coffee if you stay under budget. One friend of mine started tracking expenses with sticky notes and managed to pay off her $800 credit card bill in six months simply by identifying where her cash was slipping away and adjusting a few habits. Every little bit counts; small wins pile up until suddenly you're in control, and that's a total upgrade from barely scraping by.

Understanding Paychecks, Taxes, and Withholding

	Current			YTD	
	Hours/Units	Rate	Amount	Hours/Units	Amount
Earnings	**80.0000**		**$3,393.46**	**1,200.0000**	**$56,601.75**
Regular	80.0000	42.4183	$3,393.46	1,080.0000	$45,811.71
Paid Time Off				64.0000	$2,714.76
Holiday				56.0000	$2,375.43
Seasonal Bonus					$5,699.85
Taxable Benefits			**$8.39**		**$117.46**
Group Term Life			$8.39		$117.46
Memo Information			**$122.63**		**$1,989.62**
HSA ER			$20.83		$291.62
401K Roth ER			$101.80		$1,698.00
Pre-Tax Deductions			**$142.85**		**$1,999.90**
Dental Pretax			$11.83		$165.62
Med Pretax			$106.53		$1,491.42
Vision Pretax			$3.66		$51.24
HSA Self			$20.83		$291.62
Taxes			**$650.65**		**$11,491.37**
Federal			$401.33		$7,305.34
Social Security			$202.06		$3,392.60
Medicare			$47.26		$793.43
Post-Tax Deductions			**$302.75**		**$4,965.97**
Critical Illnes			$18.50		$259.00
401K ROTH			$271.48		$4,528.19
Group Accident			$2.69		$37.66
Hospital			$10.08		$141.12
			Amount		Amount
Net Pay			**$2,297.21**		**$38,144.51**

It's payday. You're feeling rich...until you open your pay stub and see a chunk missing. Suddenly, your "I'm going to treat myself" plans turn into "Maybe I'll just get the plain coffee." If you've ever stared at those numbers and acronyms like they're written in ancient runes, you're not alone. Let's break it down. At the top, you'll see your gross pay. That's the total amount you earned before anything gets taken out. Unfortunately, that number looks way better than what you actually get. At the bottom is net pay, which is what lands in your bank account after deductions.

Deductions can include federal and state taxes, Social Security, Medicare, and other expenses such as retirement contributions or health insurance. Then there's "year-to-date" (YTD), which means how much you've made (and how much has been taken out) so far this year. You might spot codes like FICA (representing Social Security and Medicare combined) or abbreviations for various taxes and benefits. Each section tells a little story about where your money went—sometimes it's a comedy, sometimes a tragedy.

Where Did All My Money Go? Taxes.

Taxes are the main reason your paycheck feels lighter than expected. The government takes out federal income tax based on your earnings and the info you gave your employer when you started. Some states, and even cities, add their own taxes, so if you're working in a spot with local taxes, expect to see another deduction line. Most of these are calculated automatically, but it helps to know why they're there. Basically, the government doesn't trust us to send in our taxes ourselves, so they deduct them before we can even consider spending money on video games.

When you started your job, you probably filled out a W-4 form. This piece of paper decides how much tax gets taken out of each paycheck. If you claimed more dependents or allowances, less tax comes out now, but you might owe money at tax time. If you claim fewer dependents, more money will be taken out now, and you might receive a refund later. You can check or change your W-4 anytime—just ask your HR or payroll person for the form or update it online if your company is fancy like that. It's not as scary as it sounds: Fill in your name, address, and Social Security number (don't lose this form), then answer the questions about dependents (kids or sometimes roommates who eat all your snacks...but mostly just kids). If your life changes—a new job, a new apartment, or you suddenly become a parent—update your W-4 so your paycheck doesn't surprise you later.

Necessary tax forms are like Pokémon: You gotta catch 'em all. W-2 forms arrive after New Year's from any job where you were an employee the previous year—they show how much you made and what got withheld for taxes. If you freelance, drive for apps, or do side gigs, you'll receive a 1099 instead, which means taxes weren't with-held, and you need to set aside money to pay those taxes come April (self-control level: expert). Mark your calendar: Employers must send W-2s by January 31. Toss them in a folder labeled "tax stuff" (phys-ical or digital) so that you won't have to tear apart your room to find them when taxes are due in April. Even if you're just working part-time or doing side gigs between classes, these documents matter for filing taxes or for showing proof of income to landlords or loan folks who want to know you can pay rent without selling your sneaker collection. Set reminders for tax season (April 15 for most people), and keep any paperwork that looks important, even if it's to feel like a real adult for a minute.

Documents Needed for Tax Preparation

- **Business income and expenses**
- **Form 1095-A (if applicable)**
- **Income statements (W-2s, 1099s, etc.)**
- **Interest statements**
- **Investment income**
- **Medical expense records**
- **Photo ID**
- **Prior year's tax return**
- **Property tax statements**
- **Records of charitable donations**
- **Social Security card**
- **Student loan info**

Choosing and Managing Your First Checking and Savings Accounts

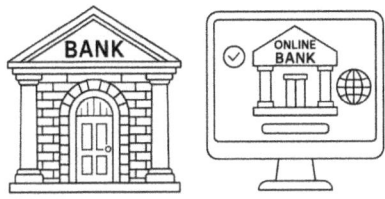

Picking your first bank account is kind of like picking your first real apartment—location, fees, and weird hidden rules all matter. You've got choices: local banks, online banks, and credit unions. Local banks are like that little coffee shop on the corner—familiar with in-person service, but sometimes they charge more fees. Credit unions? Think "community vibes," not-for-profit, often lower fees, sometimes trickier to join unless you live in the correct zip code or work for a particular company. Online banks are digital-first ninjas—no branches, lower fees, and apps that actually work, but forget about walking in for help if you lose your debit card. For young adults, no-fee checking accounts are a must. Look for ones that do not have monthly charges or minimum balance requirements. Otherwise, your so-called free checking could turn into a slow-draining money pit. Digital perks matter too: Mobile check deposit means you can cash birthday checks in your pajamas, and Zelle or Venmo integrations let you pay back friends fast when you "forget" your wallet at wing night.

Opening an Account

Opening an account isn't rocket science, but you do need a few things on hand. Bring a government-issued ID (your driver's license or passport), your Social Security number, and something with your address on it—a bill, utility payment, lease, or even a piece of official mail—that proves you live where you say you live. Ask the banker (or online chat) about overdraft policies and minimum balance traps, those sneaky rules where you get dinged $10 for dropping below a certain amount. If you're leaning toward online banking, you'll snap photos of your ID and upload them. If you are banking in person, they'll make copies. Be wary of "free gifts" for opening an account; those can be bait for accounts with hidden fees.

Once you've set up your account, managing it effectively is what keeps the money flowing in the right direction rather than evaporating into thin air. Enroll in online banking immediately—seriously, don't wait for the paper statements to arrive as if it were still 2005. Set up direct deposit if your employer offers it; your paycheck lands faster, and you skip the line at the bank. Get familiar with ATM rules. Some banks charge you for using out-of-network machines, so find the free ATMs near you or download their locator app before you're stranded at 2 a.m. with $3 in quarters. To avoid accidental overdrafts (and those gnarly $35 fees), sign up for low-balance alerts on your phone. They'll ping you when your account dips too low, so you can stop spending before things get ugly.

Linking accounts and using payment apps is a modern must. Venmo, PayPal, and Apple Pay make splitting bills or paying rent painless— just make sure you're connecting to verified apps, and never link to anything sketchy promising "free cash." Always set up two-factor authentication when possible so nobody drains your account while you nap. Double-check that any app you use is FDIC-insured or reputable. If an app asks for unusual information or sends suspicious emails, delete it immediately, just like an expired coupon. With these steps, your money's secure and accessible, and you're one step closer to stress-free adulting.

Smart Saving—Emergency Funds and Sinking Funds Explained

We've all been there: You're cruising through life, feeling mildly responsible, when your car coughs once and promptly refuses to start. Or you wake up with a toothache so fierce you regret every piece of Halloween candy you ever ate. Here's where an emergency fund swoops in like a financial superhero. An emergency fund is your stash of cash for genuine "oh no" moments—broken phone, surprise medical copay, sudden job loss, or when your laptop launches itself off the desk before finals. It's not for last-minute concert tickets or a midnight food delivery. The goal is to have enough to cover three-to-six months of living expenses, but let's be real—starting with $500 or even $200 is a win. The point isn't perfection; it's being ready for the unexpected without having to text your parents or max out a credit card.

Building this safety net doesn't mean skipping every coffee or living on canned beans. Start as small as you need; five bucks a week is a totally legit beginning. Most bank apps let you set up automatic transfers from checking to savings, so your cash sneaks over before you can spend it on bubble tea. Treat it like a non-negotiable bill, not an afterthought. Some apps even let you set savings goals and track your progress with satisfying visual indicators, such as little bars or confetti when you hit milestones. Watching your emergency fund grow slowly and steadily is weirdly thrilling, like leveling up in a video game but with fewer monsters and more peace of mind.

Now, there's another savings trick young adults swear by: sinking funds. Unlike emergency funds (for life's chaos), sinking funds are for expenses you can see coming from a mile away. Think holiday gifts, annual car insurance, future travel, or that inevitable laptop replacement when yours starts making sad whirring noises. Make a list of all the "big-ticket" stuff that hits once or twice a year and estimate what you'll need for each. Divide the total by how many months until the expense hits, then stash that amount each month in a separate savings bucket (many banks let you nickname sub-accounts for this exact purpose). For example, $300 for holiday gifts divided by 10 months means putting away $30 each month. When December rolls around, you're Santa with a plan, not Scrooge with credit card regrets.

Sometimes, life throws curveballs, and you're forced to dip into savings for an unplanned expense. Don't spiral! That's what your emergency stash is for. If you have to use it, take a deep breath and remember that it's not failure; it's adulting done right. After the dust settles, sketch out a realistic plan to replenish what you spent. Consider pausing extra takeout or skipping new shoes for a bit. Even if it takes months to rebuild, every deposit counts, and guilt gets you nowhere. The only bad emergency fund is the one that never exists.

Quick List: Sample Sinking Funds

- **Annual subscriptions**
- **Car insurance renewal**
- **Holiday gifts**
- **New phone or laptop**
- **Textbooks or school supplies**
- **Travel/Vacation**

Getting these funds going means fewer nasty surprises and less anxiety when those "surprise but not really" expenses come knocking.

The Basics of Credit Scores and How to Build Credit Safely

Think of your credit score as the GPA of adult life; it's a three-digit number showing how well you manage borrowed money. Lenders check it before giving you loans, apartments, or even phone plans.

The higher the score, the more they trust you; a low score can mean higher costs or more hurdles to overcome.

Five main factors shape your credit score:

1. First is payment history, which has the most significant impact. Paying bills on time helps; missing them hurts.
2. Next, the amount owed measures how much debt you carry compared to your credit limit. A smaller percentage of use is better.
3. The length of your credit history matters, too; the longer you've had credit, the better.
4. New credit tracks how often you apply for new accounts.
5. Credit mix looks at whether you have different types (credit cards, student loans, etc.).

Picture a pie chart: Payment history is the largest piece, followed by amounts owed, with the rest divided between history length, new credit, and mix.

What Shapes Your Credit Score

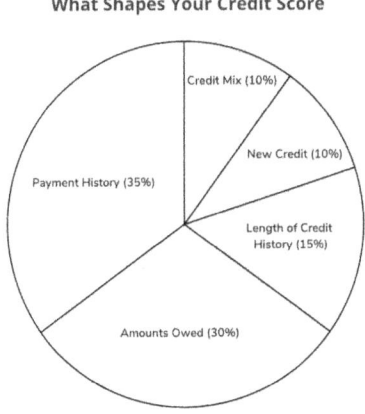

Credit Mix (10%)

New Credit (10%)

Payment History (35%)

Length of Credit History (15%)

Amounts Owed (30%)

Checking your credit score is free and won't hurt your score. You can get a free credit report each year from Experian, Equifax, and Trans-Union at AnnualCreditReport.com. Many banks and card apps also show your score. Getting your report is simple: Verify your identity and review the listed accounts and payments. If you notice anything suspicious, such as accounts you never created, report it immediately.

Building credit can feel tricky if you're starting from scratch. The safest move is a secured credit card: You deposit money as collateral and then use it like a regular card. Student cards are also good starter options and usually skip annual fees if you pay on time. Alternatively, a parent can add you as an authorized user to their card, letting you benefit from their good habits (or suffer from their bad ones, so choose wisely). Whatever card you choose, aim for one with no annual fee and low interest, and ensure the card reports activity to all three major credit bureaus. Once you open a card, use autopay to at least cover the minimum every month—no excuses.

Credit comes with traps. Late payments can damage your score for years. Maxing out your cards also looks bad; keep your balance under 30% of your limit (if you've got $1,000, don't spend more than $300). Don't open too many new accounts at once, which can make you appear risky to lenders. Chasing rewards points with too many cards or skipping payments can quickly lead to debt, and fixing the fallout takes patience and time.

Your credit score sticks with you. Sometimes it helps and sometimes it's a hassle, but it's always present. Build good habits from the start to make future financial decisions, such as buying a car or renting your dream apartment, easier.

Money alone won't solve every problem, but understanding credit makes adulthood less overwhelming. Up next: real-world spending decisions and habits that will make or break your bank account—no boring lectures needed.

Quiz:

1) What is the main difference between budgeting and expense tracking?

A. Budgeting is only used for savings, while tracking is for spending
B. Budgeting happens before you spend money, tracking happens after
C. Budgeting is more accurate than tracking
D. Expense tracking is required by law

Answer: B

Budgeting is proactive—deciding how to spend your money in advance. Tracking is reactive—reviewing where your money went afterward.

2) In the 50/30/20 budgeting method, what does the 20% represent?

A. Money for rent and groceries
B. Fun money for shopping and entertainment
C. Savings and debt repayment
D. Emergency expenses only

Answer: C

The 20% is allocated toward savings and paying off debt, helping you build financial security.

3) What is an emergency fund used for?

   A. Buying holiday gifts
   B. Planned vacations
   C. True unexpected expenses like car repairs or medical bills
   D. Paying monthly subscriptions

Answer: C

Emergency funds are meant for unplanned financial surprises—not routine or expected expenses.

4) Which of the following actions can help build a strong credit score?

   A. Maxing out your credit card for rewards
   B. Making late payments occasionally
   C. Paying bills on time and keeping balances low
   D. Opening as many credit cards as possible

Answer: C

On-time payments and keeping your credit usage low (under 30%) are key factors in maintaining a healthy credit score.

* * *

5) What is the purpose of a sinking fund?

   A. To pay off credit card debt faster
   B. To prepare for large, expected future expenses
   C. To fund emergency situations
   D. To buy stocks and investments

Answer: B

Sinking funds help you save gradually for known expenses like holidays, car repairs, or new tech, so they don't catch you off guard.

Chapter 4

Everyday Spending and Money Habits

Grocery Shopping on a Budget—Meal Prep, Lists, and Hacks

Let's face it: Grocery shopping as a young adult can feel like a chaotic adventure, with temptations lurking in every aisle. You enter determined to eat healthy and save, but often leave with a random mix of snacks, wilted lettuce, and a receipt that makes you rethink your decisions. Grocery stores are designed to lure you into impulse purchases with flashy displays and "limited edition" treats. However, with some preparation and persistence, you can outsmart these traps and stay on budget.

There's a simple game changer: meal planning before you shop. Instead of aimlessly wandering the store, go in with a plan. Meal planning saves money, reduces food waste, and ensures you have complete meals, not just random condiments and snacks. Create a simple weekly meal plan. No need to be a chef; just pick basic, cheap dinners—for example, roasted chicken with potatoes and carrots, pasta with sauce and spinach, or black bean quesadillas with salsa. Mix and match these meals, add simple breakfasts like oatmeal or eggs, and repeat a couple of lunches for the week. Your week has structure, and you avoid desperate fridge raids at midnight.

Before shopping, check what you already have at home. Take inventory of your fridge and pantry to avoid buying duplicates, like that third jar of peanut butter hiding in the back. Write down what's running low or needed, and build your grocery list and meal plan around what you already have. This alone can cut your grocery bill by 10–20% and help you use up items that might otherwise go to waste.

Treat your grocery list as your financial defense. Sort the list by category: produce, dairy, grains, protein, and snacks. This keeps your trip efficient and helps avoid money-wasting detours down tempting aisles. Stick to the list and avoid browsing for fun. If it's not on the list, it's probably an impulse buy. Know the difference between staples (foods you buy regularly, such as rice, eggs, bread, beans, and pasta) and the fun, unnecessary extras (such as neon cereal or that trendy new soda). Never shop when you're hungry. Shopping on an empty stomach almost always leads to a cart full of snacks and regret.

Pro Tip: Buy Produce That's in Season

Out-of-season items, such as strawberries in winter, are often overpriced; seasonal produce is typically cheaper and fresher. Take advantage of store discounts on fruits or veggies that are currently plentiful, and use these deals to guide your meal planning. Off-season produce is often more expensive because it's shipped from far away.

Stretch your budget by using store loyalty cards. Most grocery chains (including Kroger or Safeway) offer free membership programs with exclusive discounts. Target Circle gives access to grocery deals if you use their app or account. Store apps usually have digital coupons, so spend a minute scrolling before you shop, and you could easily save several dollars. Don't be shy about scanning discounts at checkout. Every bit adds up.

Pay attention to the "unit price" labels on store shelves. They display the cost per ounce or pound, allowing you to easily compare brands or package sizes. Sometimes, buying two smaller boxes is more cost-effective per serving than purchasing one large box. If you're unsure, use your calculator to do the math. You'll save money by paying attention to these details.

The best way to save your time and money is to shop only once a week and batch-cook when you get home. Choose one day (such as Sunday), put on some music or a podcast, and prep your meals in bulk. Cut up veggies, cook grains, and prepare proteins all at once, then divide them into meal-sized containers. Freeze portions you won't eat soon—soups, stews, and cooked meats freeze well for busy days ahead.

Basic Grocery Staples to Keep on Hand

- Bread or tortillas
- Canned beans, tuna, or soup
- Coffee or tea
- Eggs
- Fresh/frozen fruits and vegetables
- Milk (or nondairy alternative)
- Olive oil or cooking spray
- Peanut butter or nut butter
- Rice or pasta
- Salt, pepper, basic spices

Your Weekly Grocery Prep Game Plan

- **Check fridge and pantry for leftovers.**
- **Plan simple, budget-friendly dinners for the week.**
- **Organize a grocery list by category.**
- **Eat before heading out to avoid impulse buys.**

- **Sign up for store loyalty apps and deals.**
- **Compare unit prices to get the best value.**
- **Stick to your list and skip the unnecessary extras.**
- **Batch-prep meals after shopping.**
- **Freeze leftovers for easy future meals.**

Once you start planning and shopping this way, you're running your kitchen like a savvy manager. Every smart choice means less wasted food, healthier meals, and more cash left for what really matters (including, yes, better snacks).

Outsmarting Lifestyle Creep and Social Spending Pressure

Lifestyle creep is the sneaky villain lurking in your wallet. At first, you're cautious, making coffee at home, walking instead of using Uber, and holding off on buying new shoes. Then comes a raise or some side income, and suddenly, your spending quietly climbs. Lattes become a daily treat, ride-shares replace the bus, and streaming subscriptions multiply. No one plans to go broke; it's a series of minor upgrades that build up before you notice. Only when you compare your past expenses with your current ones do you realize your savings haven't increased—even with a higher income—because your spending has grown just as fast. Rent, groceries, and one streaming service turn into rent plus gym memberships, fancy takeout, and pricier clothes. The extra money didn't disappear; it just transformed into new "needs."

Social pressure is a different challenge. It's easy to go from "I'll pass" to "Sure, let's split the bill for sushi." Friends may not see how their preferred plans drain your account. Social media amplifies the problem; endless brunch and concert posts spark a sense of FOMO. You want to join in, but your budget says no. The solution? Be upfront:

"I'm saving right now. Want to do something low-key this weekend?" or "Let's do a movie night at my place." Most people get it. In fact, many are relieved to spend less. If it feels awkward turning down plans, shift your approach: "That spot looks cool, but my budget's tight. How about a potluck or park hangout?" Setting boundaries so you aren't left with an empty wallet before payday is a smart approach to budgeting.

Peer pressure also comes in the form of kindness or "treat yourself" encouragement. The "you deserve it!" mindset is everywhere. Yes, you deserve nice things, but not all at once. When someone says, "You only live once!" you can calmly reply, "True, but I'm picking my YOLO moments carefully." For pricey group activities, suggest creative cost-cutting measures, such as having everyone bring a dish or rotating hosting responsibilities. If someone insists on expensive plans, it's fair to say, "That's out of my range this time. I'll join the next one."

Tracking Purchases and Understanding Priorities

Defining your personal spending priorities is like a cheat code for adulting. Ask yourself: *What actually feels worth it? What's just FOMO?* Spend a week tracking purchases—note which ones bring joy and which end in regret. Maybe your takeaway is that lattes spark happiness, but new clothes offer little excitement after the first wear. Or maybe that travel means more than bar tabs. Once you see patterns, jot them down in a "Worth It" worksheet with two columns —spending that genuinely adds to your life versus what you do just because others are. Review the list when temptation strikes or social invitations pile up.

You don't have to skip fun to save. Just get creative. Budget-friendly swaps keep you social without overspending. Instead of going to bars every weekend, host a game night or a movie marathon at home. Ask guests to bring snacks or drinks so it feels special but affordable. If your group loves to shop, visit thrift stores instead of malls; it becomes a treasure hunt and is cheaper than fast fashion (plus, the styles are more unique). When everyone is excited about a concert, seek out local music nights or free events. They're often just as entertaining for a fraction of the price.

Try thrifting to discover unique finds and find funky bargains. You can build a great wardrobe for much less and sometimes even find designer labels for next to nothing. Try organizing clothing swaps; everyone brings unused items and leaves with something "new." It's an easy, free way to satisfy shopping cravings.

It also helps to have quick responses for tricky spending moments. If someone pitches a pricey idea, say: "Sounds fun, but I'm on a budget. Can we grab coffee instead?" When the group wants to split an uneven bill, you might say, "I only had the salad and water, so I'll just pay for mine." If anyone protests, remember—it's your money and your choice.

In the end, resisting lifestyle creep and social pressure comes down to knowing yourself and what's truly important, not what looks best online or what your friends splurge on. Intentional spending means sometimes saying no, but more importantly, saying yes to what you truly value, whether that's saving for a trip, investing in hobbies, or just knowing you have peace of mind with savings in the bank.

Subscriptions, Streaming, and Recurring Costs—Spotting Sneaky Expenses

Recurring expenses are stealthy; they quietly auto-renew and chip away at your balance before you notice. Many people have discovered random charges, such as $12.99 for a forgotten service, on their statements. Like laundry socks, these charges often multiply unnoticed. The first defense is simple: Become your own expense detective. Review your past few months of bank and credit card statements line by line. Highlight all recurring charges, such as Netflix, Spotify, cloud storage, fitness apps, or old "Pro" memberships that you rarely use. Though it may feel tedious, seeing those \$4.99 or \$14.99 charges stacked up is an eye-opener.

Tech can help if manual scans feel overwhelming. Subscription-tracking apps like Trim or Hiatus connect to your accounts and identify recurring charges, including forgotten services such as a meditation app from a stressful week or a streaming platform for a single show. These apps list every subscription, warn you of price hikes, highlight duplicates, and sometimes let you cancel with just a tap. They'll often break down your total subscription spending, revealing the actual cost of all those "free trials" you forgot to cancel.

Reviewing subscriptions feels a lot like cleaning your closet—you'll rediscover things you haven't used in ages. The trick is to assess, not just list, what stays and what goes. Try a 30-day challenge: Track how often you use each service. Do you listen to Spotify Premium every day, or can you tolerate some ads? Is Disney+ collecting dust while you're always on YouTube? After a month, keep only those you actually use. Unused subscriptions are like gym memberships for non-gym-goers: They sound good in theory, but they can drain your wallet if ignored.

Beware of Free Trials and Hidden Fees

Free trials are infamous for silently converting to paid plans. Mark their end dates on your calendar as soon as you sign up. Use your phone's reminder app to get notified before your card is charged. If you're testing Spotify or Netflix, set an alert two days before your renewal with the service name and login credentials. That way, you'll get to decide whether to keep or cancel right on time. Some cancellation processes are hidden; if you can't find the button, check the help page for instructions.

Watch out for hidden fees, as some services charge extra for "premium" access or add taxes not disclosed upfront. Always read the fine print before you subscribe. If there's an annual discount that jumps to a higher rate on renewal, note that date so you aren't surprised down the line.

Negotiating or downgrading subscriptions can be more effective than you think. If your internet or phone bill suddenly jumps, don't just accept it; call and ask about promotions or consider keeping your old rate. Be polite but direct: "Hi, I noticed my bill increased this month. Are there any ways to lower it or any new promos?" Providers often offer secret deals or student rates if you ask—sometimes up to half off for students or those under 26.

Here is a sample (and simple) negotiation script: "I'm considering switching unless there's a better offer," or "My budget is tight—is there a cheaper plan I can move to?" Customer service reps are accustomed to these questions and often have discounts or extra months of service to offer if you appear ready to cancel or switch.

For streaming, switching to a family plan with friends or siblings can make each person's cost cheaper. When sharing, trustworthiness is key to avoiding drama over account access.

Don't ignore bundle deals. Many mobile or internet companies will cut monthly costs if you combine services (phone + internet + streaming). Only bundle if you use every included service; otherwise, stick to what fits your lifestyle.

Periodically review your subscriptions—set a reminder every quarter to check your list. Needs change: Maybe you finished watching everything on one platform or switched gyms. Cancel anything unused and direct those funds to savings or things that make you happier. Every dollar saved can go toward trips, hobbies, or simply reducing monthly financial stress.

Quick-Action Exercise: Subscription Spring Cleaning

List every recurring charge on your two most recent statements (streaming, cloud storage, delivery memberships, etc.). Next to each, note how many times

you used it last month. Circle anything unused or over-priced. Cancel at least one service today or downgrade to a lower-tier plan. Set a calendar reminder to redo this review in three months.

First-Time Big Purchases—Phones, Laptops, and Furniture

Nothing feels more grown-up than the moment you start thinking about buying big-ticket stuff with your own cash. Suddenly, you're researching phones, scoping out laptops, and scrolling endless furniture listings, all while wondering if you'll still have money for rent. It's stressful, exciting, and a little bit scary. The trick is knowing how to make these choices without falling for shiny marketing or blowing your entire savings on a mattress that promises to "change your life." Let's break it down, step by step, so you don't end up with buyer's remorse or a couch that smells like regret.

Using a Decision Matrix

When you're faced with the urge to buy something major, use a decision matrix, which is simply a fancy way of weighing "need" against "want," comparing features, and checking what really fits your budget. Start by asking yourself whether this is something you really need right now. For example, if your laptop dies in the middle of finals week, that's a need. If your phone works fine, but the new model just dropped with 10 more cameras, that's a want. List out the features that matter most—battery life, speed, storage, warranty—and ignore the hype about things you'll never use (do you really need a phone that tracks your sleep cycle and makes pancakes?). Then, compare options side by side. Sometimes, refurbished electronics make more sense than buying new ones. Take laptops, for example: A refurbished model from a reputable store usually comes with a warranty and costs less than half the price of a new one. Here's a quick sample comparison:

Feature	Refurbished Laptop	New Laptop
Price	Around $400	Around $900
Warranty	1-year warranty	1-year warranty
Condition	Minor cosmetic wear	Brand new, no signs of use
Latest-Model?	Not always the newest version	Usually the latest model
Eco-Friendly?	Yes - promotes reuse	Not particularly eco-friendly

When buying furniture, be realistic about what you need now and what can wait. Maybe you need a bed frame so you're not sleeping on the floor, but that $300 coffee table can stay on the wish list. Second-hand options on Facebook Marketplace or local thrift shops are solid picks for stuff like desks or chairs. Always inspect photos closely and ask about any mystery stains or wobbly legs before making a purchase.

Budgeting for significant buys is non-negotiable if you want to avoid debt. Create a sinking fund—basically, set aside a little bit each week or month so you're not scrambling when it's time to pay up. Most mobile banking apps allow you to create savings goals with cute names, such as "Laptop Fund" or "Escape Old Futon." Set an end date and divide the total cost by the number of months until then. Watching your progress bar fill up feels like unlocking an achievement in real life. I remember saving for my first solo trip. Each time my fund grew, so did my confidence. It was proof I could plan ahead and stick to a goal.

Before you fork over cash for anything significant, watch out for red flags. If the price seems too good to be true, it probably is. Scams are everywhere, especially online. Always meet sellers in public places if possible. For electronics, ask about the item's age, whether it comes with a charger, and if there's visible damage. Look for seller reviews or ratings if buying through an app. For used furniture, sit on it (if possible) and check for unusual smells, stains, or damaged parts. Also, ask about pets or smoking in the home, as you don't want to bring any surprises back to your apartment. Check if there's a return policy or at least some kind of agreement if the item isn't as described.

Warranties and Insurance

Warranties and insurance can be lifesavers for expensive gadgets. Many stores offer student discounts—Apple and Best Buy, for example, both have deals available if you show your student ID or sign in with your school email. Sometimes, these discounts knock off enough money to make the "new" price almost as cheap as a used one. Always register new electronics for warranty coverage immediately after purchase; it takes just five minutes, but can save you hundreds if something breaks down. If insurance is offered for items like phones or laptops and you're accident-prone (no shame), consider adding it, especially if it's cheap or bundled with your phone plan.

Look for discount codes before checking out; browser extensions like Honey or Rakuten will automatically scour the web for deals. Many credit cards also offer purchase protection or extended warranties on items bought with the card, so check your app or call customer service to see what's included.

To sum it up: Evaluate what you truly need versus what looks cool in ads; compare all your options using a simple table or checklist; plan your purchase by saving up instead of swiping credit impulsively; watch out for scams and sketchy sellers when shopping used; and take advantage of every discount, warranty, or protection plan available to keep your stuff safe.

Big purchases don't have to feel overwhelming or risky when you approach them methodically and patiently. Learning to weigh options and plan ahead doesn't just save money; it builds real confidence in your ability to handle life's bigger challenges.

Now that you've built money smarts for everything from groceries to gadgets, it's time to turn your attention to what's happening in your kitchen. This next chapter is all about smart cooking and basic nutrition, skills that fuel your body and boost your independence. After all, nothing says "I've got this" like whipping up a healthy meal without relying on takeout or microwave dinners!

Quiz:

1) What's one smart strategy to reduce impulse buys at the grocery store?

   A. Shopping late at night when fewer people are around
   B. Writing your grocery list in alphabetical order
   C. Shopping on an empty stomach so you'll move faster
   D. Eating before shopping and sticking to a categorized list

Answer: D

Eating before you shop helps prevent impulse snacking, and a categorized list keeps you focused and efficient.

* * *

2) What is lifestyle creep?

   A. When your cost of living rises due to inflation
   B. When your income goes down but spending stays the same
   C. When spending increases as your income rises, often unconsciously
   D. When friends borrow money and don't pay it back

Answer: C

Lifestyle creep is the gradual increase in spending when income goes up, often leading to little or no increase in savings.

* * *

3) How can you stay on top of recurring subscription charges?

A. Wait for your bank to alert you
B. Use tracking apps like Trim or manually review your bank statements
C. Cancel every subscription after one month
D. Subscribe with different emails to get free trials repeatedly

Answer: B

Subscription tracking apps and manual reviews help you catch unused or duplicate subscriptions draining your account.

* * *

4) What's the purpose of a decision matrix when making big purchases?

A. To guess how long you'll use an item
B. To determine your monthly payment plan
C. To compare needs vs. wants and evaluate key features
D. To find the trendiest brands to buy

Answer: C

A decision matrix helps compare features, prices, and prioritize needs over wants before committing to a big expense.

* * *

5) Which of the following is a helpful way to resist social spending pressure?

   A. Always carry cash so you can say you forgot your card
   B. Tell friends you're broke even if you're not
   C. Offer budget-friendly alternatives like a potluck or movie night
   D. Avoid all social invitations

Answer: C

Suggesting low-cost alternatives helps you stay social without blowing your budget or feeling left out.

* * *

Chapter 5

Smart Cooking and Nutrition for Beginners

Essential Kitchen Tools—What You Really Need (And What You Don't)

At one time or another, most of us have wished dinner would magically appear, especially when facing a counter filled with takeout boxes. I once used a coffee mug and toaster for grilled cheese (I don't recommend it). But the real secret? You don't need shelves of gadgets or "as seen on TV" tools to cook real food. A good starter kitchen contains a handful of essentials, not overfilled drawers with avocado pitters and banana slicers. Less clutter means less stress (and more money in your pocket).

First, get a chef's knife—it's the MVP of your kitchen. It chops, slices, dices, and even tackles tough veggies. Choose one that feels sturdy and comfortable, but you don't need to splurge. Avoid anything flimsy or made of plastic. Next, grab a plastic or bamboo cutting board; they're easy to clean and won't dull your knife. A medium saucepan with a lid is your go-to for boiling pasta, soup, or rice. Lids trap heat and keep food from jumping out when you're distracted by your phone.

A nonstick skillet is ideal for cooking eggs, pancakes, grilled cheese, and stir-fry. Choose one with a balanced feel and a handle that stays cool. A sheet pan (also known as a baking tray) is a must for roasting veggies, baking proteins, or even making cookies. Measuring cups and spoons prevent breakfast disasters where "eyeballing" leads to concrete-like oats. Toss in a mixing bowl for salads, beating eggs, or popcorn on movie night. With these basics, you can cook almost anything.

Now, what can wait? Garlic presses are just extra cleanup (a knife will do). Avocado slicers are fun but rarely necessary (spoons and knives work just as well). Rice cookers are handy for large batches or if you eat rice often, but a pot works fine otherwise. Skip single-use tools like egg separators or strawberry hullers unless you bake daily or compete in fruit-carving competitions.

You don't need to spend a fortune on quality. Thrift stores often have almost new gear; many people donate unused gifts from wedding registries. Discount stores (like T.J. Maxx or Marshalls) sell good cookware on a budget. Choose knives with solid, weighted handles (flimsy knives are frustrating and less safe), and look for cookware with no loose handles or deep scratches on nonstick surfaces (nobody wants mystery flakes in their meals). Try to avoid warped pans, as well.

The Importance of Kitchen Safety

A little kitchen safety will save your fingers and keep your tools in shape. Always hand-wash knives—dishwashers dull blades and damage handles. Hold knives by the dull top edge, not the sharp side. Dry them immediately to prevent rust, then store knives in a block or on a magnetic strip rather than tossing them into a drawer. Avoid stacking nonstick pans if possible; placing a towel between each pan works wonders.

Regularly sharpening your chef's knife will make cooking smoother and safer (no more squished tomatoes). Honing a basic steel every few weeks works well, and numerous quick tutorials are available online. Scrub cutting boards with hot, soapy water after each use—no one wants yesterday's onion in today's fruit.

Your Starter Kitchen Kit

- **Chef's knife**
- **Cutting board**
- **Measuring cups and spoons**
- **Medium saucepan with lid**
- **Mixing bowl**
- **Nonstick skillet**
- **Sheet pan**

That's all you really need. Skip the clutter and stick to gear that makes cooking genuinely easier. Your future self (and your budget) will thank you.

Cooking 101—Mastering Five Basic Techniques Every Adult Needs

Cooking isn't only for reality TV stars or grandmas. It's a life skill built on a handful of basic moves that can unlock endless meal options. Here's how to master the essentials.

1. **Boiling** seems simple, but it often trips people up, especially with pasta. To do it right, fill a pot with water, season it well with salt, and bring it to a rolling boil. Add noodles, stir so they don't clump, and start checking doneness a minute or two before the box says—*al dente* is cooked through with a little bite. Keep your eyes on the water, as it will boil over if the stove is too hot. For eggs, gently lower them into simmering water (not boiling) and cook for about 10 minutes for hard yolks. A green ring around the yolk just means it's overcooked, not that it's

unsafe to eat. Use tongs or a spoon to handle hot eggs and avoid burns.

2. **Roasting** is a set-it-and-forget-it method perfect for any hearty vegetable or chicken. Chop the veggies, toss them with oil and seasoning, and spread them out on a baking sheet. Roast in a hot oven (425 °F/220 °C) for 25–40 minutes. Flip halfway so both sides cook evenly and don't stick. When roasting chicken, follow the same principles and check doneness by looking for clear juices. If veggies are mushy, try spreading them out more or using a hotter oven. Always use real oven mitts, not dish towels.

3. **Sautéing** basically means frying ingredients quickly in a skillet. Heat a slick of oil until shimmering, then add aromatics like onions or garlic first (garlic cooks faster than onions, so put that in last before adding the main dish). Once fragrant, add other veggies, stirring often. If things stick or brown too quickly, turn down the heat; if they're soggy, increase the heat in the pan next time. Avoid crowding the pan. For a starter recipe, sauté sliced peppers and onions with salt until soft and slightly browned—great for tacos or sandwiches.

4. **Baking** isn't just for cookies. Sheet-pan meals are dinners in disguise. Lay out chicken breasts, brush them with oil, sprinkle with seasoning, and bake at 400 °F (205 °C) for 20–25 minutes (the juices should run clear, and the meat should feel firm). Overbake, and the meat goes dry; underbake, and it's dangerous. Grab a cheap meat thermometer and aim for 165 °F (74 °C).

5. **Steaming** preserves color in vegetables and keeps dumplings soft. Use a steamer basket over simmering water, or improvise with a metal colander and pot with a lid. Broccoli usually takes about five minutes—poke with a fork for crisp-tender results. Oversteam, and you'll get mushy

vegetables. When lifting lids, open them away from your face to avoid steam burns.

Mistakes happen to everyone. If you burn food, scrape off the over-done parts (unless it's pure charcoal, in which case, toss it), and soak pans now to save scrubbing later. When handling raw meat, please wash your hands and cutting surfaces, and do not reuse plates that hold it until they've been thoroughly cleaned.

Quick Reference: Gateway Recipes for Each Technique

- **Boiling: Hard-boiled eggs—cover with water, bring to a boil, cover, turn off heat, and wait 10 minutes. Remove from hot water and cool off in some ice water.**
- **Roasting: Potatoes with oil and rosemary— roast at 425 °F until golden.**
- **Sautéing: Bell peppers and onions in hot oil— cook until soft and caramelized.**
- **Baking: Chicken breasts brushed with oil and spices—bake at 400 °F until juices run clear.**
- **Steaming: Place broccoli florets in a steamer basket over simmering water, cover, and steam for 5 minutes.**

Mastering these five techniques makes cooking far less intimidating, and you might even start to enjoy your time in the kitchen.

Simple, Nutritious Meals—No Experience Required

Cooking at home doesn't mean sacrificing your free time, spending a fortune, or acquiring a culinary degree. You can whip up real food using basic ingredients, minimal effort, and—most importantly— without burning down your kitchen.

A Simple Stir-Fry

Let's start with a three-ingredient stir fry. Grab a bag of frozen mixed veggies, some rice (leftover or freshly cooked), and soy sauce. Heat a skillet over medium, toss in the veggies straight from the freezer, and cook until hot and just tender. Add rice, splash with soy sauce, and stir until everything is steamy. If you want to jazz it up, toss in left-over chicken, tofu, or even an egg. Hot sauce or fresh herbs like cilantro give it a new vibe.

One-Pot Chili

For something hearty, try a one-pot chili. In a big pot, cook chopped onion (or skip if you're anti-onion), a can of beans (any kind), canned tomatoes, and chili powder. Simmer until thick. Ground turkey or beef works if you want to add meat; just brown it first. If you're on a budget or a vegetarian, double the beans or add corn. Taste and adjust the seasoning—cumin or paprika are fun, so add some if you have them.

Sheet-Pan Fajitas

Sheet-pan fajitas require almost no brainpower. Slice bell peppers and onions (don't cry, it gets better), and toss them on a baking tray with strips of chicken, or even canned chickpeas for a plant-based version. Sprinkle with oil, salt, pepper, and a dash of chili powder. Bake at 400 °F until everything is browned and sizzling, usually 20–25 minutes. Pile into tortillas with salsa or a squeeze of lime, and call it dinner.

Simple Breakfasts: Oats and Parfait

Breakfast doesn't have to mean dry cereal forever. Overnight oats take just three minutes to prepare: Mix rolled oats with milk (dairy or nondairy), a spoonful of yogurt, and a splash of honey in a jar or bowl. Stir, cover, and refrigerate overnight. In the morning, add fruit or nuts for a crunchy texture. If you want something more dessert-like, try Greek yogurt parfaits: Layer yogurt with berries and granola or even crushed-up cereal. It's breakfast you can assemble half-asleep.

Superhero Eggs

Eggs are budget superheroes. A veggie omelet is as easy as beating two eggs with a pinch of salt, pouring them into a hot nonstick pan, and adding whatever's hanging out in your fridge—cheese, spinach, tomatoes—before folding it in half when the bottom sets. Don't stress about perfect technique; even an ugly omelet tastes great.

Pro Tip: Egg Freshness Test

Place the egg in a bowl of cold water:

- **Sinks and lies flat on its side = very fresh**
- **Sinks but stands upright = still okay, but use soon**
- **Floats to the top = don't eat it**

The Unbeatable Quesadilla

Bean-and-cheese quesadillas are unbeatable for late-night cravings or lunch on the go. Spread canned beans (refried or drained black beans) on half of a tortilla, sprinkle with cheese, fold over, and cook in a skillet until golden brown. Flip carefully—a spatula helps—and repeat for the second side. Slice into wedges and dip in salsa.

All these recipes level up easily. You can substitute lentils for beans in chili or toss leftover roasted veggies into your stir-fry. Fajitas become spicier with jalapeños or milder with sour cream. Omelets welcome any leftover meat, or even cooked potatoes. Chili becomes heartier with the addition of quinoa or rice stirred in at the end.

Make sure you have a good place to store your leftovers. Transfer food to clean containers as soon as it's cool—don't leave it on the stove for hours unless you want to meet new bacteria. Slap on a piece of tape and label it with the date (yes, you'll forget when you made it).

Most meals last three to four days in the fridge; if you don't eat them that quickly, consider freezing them for later. When reheating, use the microwave for speed—cover loosely to prevent splattering—or gently warm on the stove with a splash of water to prevent the food from drying out.

Quick Reference: Reheating and Storage Tips

- **Eat refrigerated food within 3–4 days.**
- **Freeze extras if not eating soon.**
- **Label leftovers with the date.**
- **Microwave: Stir halfway through for even heating.**
- **Store meals in airtight containers.**
- **Stovetop: Add a splash of liquid to prevent sticking.**

Trying these recipes quickly builds confidence, and suddenly, home-cooked meals feel less like a chore and more like a small victory every day.

Meal Planning and Batch Cooking for Busy Weeks

That all-too-familiar moment when your fridge holds nothing but half a jar of pickles and wilted lettuce? That's what meal planning saves you from. Instead of facing empty shelves or relying on takeout, having a plan cuts stress, saves money, and keeps last-minute, less healthy choices at bay. With some foresight, you'll skip those drive-thru stops after long days and avoid unbalanced, thrown-together meals.

Weekly meal planning is simpler than it sounds; you don't need fancy tools or chef skills. Use a basic template: Choose two breakfast options, two lunch options, three dinner options, and a couple of snack options. Breakfast might consist of oatmeal and eggs; lunch could alternate between turkey wraps and leftover pasta; and dinner might include stir-fry, tacos, and baked chicken with vegetables. Snacks could be hummus with carrots or a handful of nuts. This approach adds variety without overcomplicating things and avoids falling into the "what should I cook?" trap. Remember: When you're busy, simplicity is often the best approach.

Keeping Meals Balanced

When planning meals, focus on balance by including protein (such as chicken, beans, yogurt, and eggs), fiber (from whole grains, vegetables, and fruit), and healthy fats (such as avocado, olive oil, and nuts). Protein fills you up and helps muscles, fiber keeps your system in check and your appetite stable, and healthy fats add flavor and help you absorb nutrients. There's no need for nutrition math; just glance at your meal and check for a bit of each.

Batch Cooking Basics

Batch cooking means preparing in quantity once and eating multiple times. Make a large pot of rice or beans on Sunday to use throughout the week in burritos, grain bowls, or a quick soup. Roast a tray of veggies (maybe carrots, broccoli, and peppers) to add to salads, pasta, or dinners as needed. Make extra chicken breasts to slice for sandwiches, dice for salads, or add to stir-fries. You can even double up a chili or stew, freezing half for a night when you're really pressed for time.

Storage and Prep Tips

Effective storage keeps batch-cooked food fresh and safe to eat. Cool cooked food quickly—don't leave it out for more than two hours. Use shallow containers for faster chilling and opt for clear or labeled containers to prevent food from being forgotten. Storing cooked grains, veggies, and proteins separately allows for easy mixing and matching later. Always label with the date to avoid consuming anything questionable.

Snacks also benefit from being prepared ahead. Pre-chop veggies (store wet ones, such as carrots or celery, in water-filled jars to keep them crisp) and portion out trail mix or similar snacks for easy, healthy snacking.

How to Keep It Interesting

Batch cooking isn't boring; you just need to get creative with your components. That oven-roasted sweet potato can turn up in tacos one night, curry the next, and salad later on. Rice can evolve from a stir-fry base to fried rice or add heft to soups by the end of the week. Change sauces or seasonings to keep leftovers feeling new.

Food Safety Musts

Food safety is crucial. Always refrigerate cooked food within two hours, and eat leftovers within three to four days. Mark the freeze date on any items stored for extended periods; most cooked batch dishes are best consumed within two months. Thoroughly reheat all hot foods, especially meats and anything with eggs or dairy. Never refreeze food once thawed unless you've fully cooked it again.

With a little planning and batch cooking, your week flows more smoothly, your wallet benefits, and your meals improve from "uhh..." to "I actually made this!"

Reading Nutrition Labels and Making Healthier Swaps

Nutrient	Amount	% Daily Value
Serving Size	1 cup (228g)	
Calories	250	
Total Fat	12g	15%
Saturated Fat	3g	18%
Trans Fat	0g	0%
Cholesterol	30mg	10%
Sodium	470mg	20%
Total Carbohydrate	31g	11%
Dietary Fiber	4g	14%
Total Sugars	14g	---
Added Sugars	10g	20%
Protein	5g	10%
Calcium	260mg	20%
Iron	3.6mg	20%
Potassium	240mg	6%

Ever flipped over a cereal box only to be baffled by the nutrition label? At first, decoding them might feel like reading a foreign language, but with a little know-how, labels can help you eat smarter. Start with the serving size at the top, as it's the basis for all numbers below. If the serving size is "1 cup," but you pour a giant bowl, you'll need to adjust the numbers for what you actually eat.

Next, check calories, which are the energy from one serving. It's easy to ignore when hungry, but knowing whether you're eating a light snack or half your daily calories in one sitting matters. Beneath calories, you'll find the macronutrients: fat, carbs, and protein. Not all fats are bad, but focus on keeping saturated and trans fats low for your heart's health. Carbohydrates fuel you, but too much added sugar can leave you hungry again soon. Fiber is important because it digests slowly, keeping you full longer. Protein helps with muscle repair and staves off hunger.

On the right side of the label is the "% Daily Value" (%DV). This indicates how much one serving contributes toward your daily nutrient target based on a 2,000-calorie diet (your needs may vary). If a food has 5% DV for calcium, it's low; 20% sodium is high for one food. Keep in mind that serving sizes are often smaller than you'd expect—one can of soup might be labeled as two servings, but most people eat the whole thing. Always check the package for multiple servings to avoid accidental overeating.

Keep your eyes open for label tricks. "Natural" doesn't guarantee health; it's just a buzzword. "Low-fat" versions often add sugar or artificial thickeners. "Sugar-free" isn't always calorie-free; it very well could contain sugar substitutes or alcohol, which come with their own issues. Even "whole grain" claims can be misleading if only a small amount of the grain is included. Serving sizes are often unrealistic—a bag of chips labeled as two servings is rarely shared or saved for later.

Watch for hidden sugars and sodium, which often appear under various names, such as cane syrup, fructose, honey, or "evaporated juice." If sugar ranks in the top three ingredients, you're essentially eating dessert, even if it looks healthy. Sodium, which can cause bloating or thirst, is often hidden in canned soups, frozen meals, and sauces. For example, comparing two granola bars, one might contain 7 grams of added sugar and a lengthy list of ingredients. At the same time, the healthier option limits sugar to 3 grams and lists only oats, nuts, and dried fruit as its ingredients. Aim for shorter, simpler ingredient lists with minimal added sugar.

Healthy Swaps

Making swaps doesn't mean extreme changes or surviving only on kale smoothies. Small changes matter. For instance, use brown rice instead of white for extra fiber and lasting fullness. Greek yogurt is a protein-rich alternative to sour cream, offering probiotics as well.

Replace soda with seltzer water and a splash of juice or lemon for fizzy refreshment minus the sugar.

Craving snacks? Trade regular chips for air-popped popcorn or roasted chickpeas; both are crunchy and healthier options. Choose nut butter listings that only include nuts and salt over those with added sugar or oils. Sometimes, swap ice cream for a frozen banana blended with a splash of milk—it's creamy, sweet, and simple.

With practice, reading labels becomes second nature. Soon, you'll spot marketing tricks quickly and feel empowered about what you eat. Building these habits now saves stress—and money—later.

Healthy eating doesn't have to be expensive or overwhelming. Smart label reading and simple swaps feed both your present appetite and your future well-being. Once you have these skills, the grocery store gets a lot less intimidating (just watch out for the durian fruit— approach with caution ... trust me). Next up: how to tackle home upkeep on your own, so you don't need to call your parents for every little mess.

Quiz:

1) Which of the following tools is considered essential for a beginner's kitchen?

  A. Garlic press
  B. Chef's knife
  C. Rice cooker
  D. Avocado slicer

Answer: B

A chef's knife is versatile and essential for most cooking tasks. The others are considered optional or single-use.

* * *

2) What's a major benefit of batch cooking?

   A. Reduces water usage
   B. Makes your kitchen smell better
   C. Saves time and money by prepping multiple meals at once
   D. Eliminates the need for refrigeration

Answer: C

Batch cooking streamlines your week by prepping food in advance, saving time and reducing the temptation to order takeout.

* * *

3) Which cooking technique involves high heat and quick movement in a skillet?

   A. Boiling
   B. Baking
   C. Sautéing
   D. Steaming

Answer: C

Sautéing uses a small amount of oil and high heat to cook food quickly while stirring often.

* * *

4) What's one smart grocery tip to avoid waste and overspending?

   A. Buy only frozen meals
   B. Shop every day instead of weekly
   C. Create a meal plan and inventory what you already have
      before shopping
   D. Only shop late at night for better deals

Answer: C

Checking your fridge/pantry and planning meals before shopping helps avoid duplicates and unnecessary purchases.

5) When reading a nutrition label, which of the following is a red flag for added sugar?

   A. Short ingredient list
   B. Serving size of 1 cup
   C. "Cane syrup" listed in the top three ingredients
   D. 5% daily value for fiber

Answer: C

Sugar in the top ingredients—under names like cane syrup or fructose—indicates a high sugar content, even if the product looks healthy.

* * *

Chapter 6

Home Maintenance and DIY Essentials

Creating Your First Cleaning Schedule—Daily, Weekly, and Annual Tasks

L et's face it—cleaning isn't an elite adult skill or some mystical ritual performed with groans and scrubbing. Cleaning involves dividing and conquering tasks before your bathroom turns into a failed chemistry experiment or your dust bunnies stage a coup. Not all chores are equal: Some require daily attention to prevent chaos, while others linger until the weekend, and a handful only appear a few times a year. The upside? Tackling messes in small, regular increments saves you future horror and keeps you from living in a science lab. Keep the following in mind:

- **Daily cleaning is your shield.** Wipe counters after cooking so gunk doesn't become part of the décor. Even a quick rinse and stack of dishes wards off bad smells (and gnats). Sweep or vacuum the most frequently used areas to prevent crumbs from attracting armies of ants. These small, regular actions—often just seconds or a couple of minutes at a time—keep your space company-ready and ensure your future self is happy. Yes, it's routine, but those habits stave off much bigger problems down the road.

- **Weekly chores fill in the gaps that daily cleaning misses.** Ignore these weekly tasks, and you'll be searching for "how to de-stink my towels" in no time. Deep-clean your bathroom weekly: Sinks, toilets, and showers don't clean themselves. Laundry piles up quickly, so do a load before your wardrobe becomes overwhelmed with dirt. Change sheets at least once a week to avoid bed funk. (Trust me, you'll notice the difference.) Weekly cleanups block mold, odor, and clutter from taking over. If you cohabitate, make it fun with a "cleaning party"—music on, timer set, and whoever scrubs fastest wins (loser buys lunch).

- **Annual chores are the unsung saviors.** Once a year, wash your windows (unless you prefer mysterious smudges), deep-clean appliances such as the fridge and oven, and check or replace HVAC filters. Your lungs and budget will appreciate it. Check smoke detectors and ensure that the extinguishers are actually working. Skipping these can mean expensive repairs or safety hazards. Plus, there's a certain thrill in streak-free glass and a non-mysterious-smelling fridge.

- **Why split chores by frequency?** Because it prevents messes from piling up and your stress from skyrocketing. Daily habits block pests and sticky disasters; weekly routines smash build-ups before they take hold; and yearly checkups keep bigger issues running smoothly and avert unexpected expenses. Think of it as maintaining a well-oiled machine; if you skip maintenance, everything seizes up.

- **Customize for your living style.** If you live alone, you can stretch some weekly chores or break tasks into bite-sized pieces every few days. If you have roommates, more people equals more mess, but it also means more hands. Split responsibilities before resentment grows. Make a chart or checklist of daily, weekly, and annual tasks, and divide chores based on preferences. Hate scrubbing toilets but don't mind dishes? Switch it up. Rotate jobs monthly so no one is stuck with the worst task forever.

If lists aren't your thing, weave cleaning into another routine: Wipe the counter while your coffee brews, or vacuum during TV ads. The internet brims with hacks: Dust blinds and baseboards with a dryer sheet, which has static that zaps gunk easily. Microfiber cloths keep electronics looking shiny without lint, and Magic Erasers obliterate scuff marks with just water.

Break chores into manageable bursts. Tackle cleaning in five- or ten-minute sprints. Set a timer, pick a room, play an energetic playlist, and see how much you conquer before the timer dings. Focused effort (with a clear end in sight) makes any task easier. For motivation, pair cleaning with rewards—for example, tidy the kitchen, then enjoy an episode of your favorite show.

Shared spaces cause most roommate fights, so curb conflicts with basic systems. Keep a chart (on paper or with an app like OurHome) outlining who is responsible for what and when, such as dishes for this week, trash for next week, and sweeping on Sundays. Rotate so nobody feels condemned to the same job. If someone slacks off, trade or double up next time, but talk it out before the drama becomes a flurry of passive-aggressive post-it notes.

Customizable Cleaning Checklist

Solo Living Template:

- **Daily: Wipe counters and sink, quick sweep/vacuum, wash or rinse dishes**

- **Weekly: Deep-clean bathroom, do laundry, change sheets**
- **Annual: Wash windows, deep-clean fridge/oven/microwave, replace HVAC filters, check smoke detectors/fire extinguisher**

Roommate Template:

- **Assign daily/weekly/annual chores and rotate monthly; use group chat reminders or assign points redeemable for small perks (like choosing movie night)**

Cleaning may never become "fun," but these habits and hacks keep it from stealing your energy and turn your place from a horror story to somewhere you'd actually invite people over.

DIY Fixes—Changing Light Bulbs, Unclogging Drains, and More

So, you're living on your own, and suddenly, the world expects you to know how to fix stuff—like you magically absorbed home-repair skills through Wi-Fi. I wish. The first time a light bulb fizzled out in my apartment, I stood there holding the new bulb like I was defusing a bomb. Turns out, it wasn't that hard. With a bit of guidance and a small box of basic tools, you can handle way more than you think. Here's what you need in your toolkit: a claw hammer (for loose nails or hanging art), Phillips and flathead screwdrivers (because furniture loves to loosen up), a basic socket set, a tape measure (no more guessing if that thrift-store couch will fit), an adjustable wrench, pliers, and a utility knife. I'd toss in a flashlight for peeking into dark corners, a level for less-crooked wall art, and duct tape (the fix-it answer to 60% of life's minor chaos). With these in reach, you're set for 80% of everyday repairs, whether it's tightening a loose cabinet handle or opening a battery compartment without breaking a sweat.

Your Basic Home Maintenance Tools

- **Adjustable wrench**
- **Duct tape**
- **Flashlight (with extra batteries)**
- **Hammer and nails**
- **Level**
- **Pliers**
- **Plunger**
- **Power strip or surge protector**
- **Screwdriver (flat and Phillips)**
- **Socket Set**
- **Step stool**
- **Super glue**
- **Tape measure**
- **Utility knife**

Safe Electrical Fixes

Most home fixes start with light bulbs. You'll see screw-in bulbs everywhere; twist left to remove the old one and right to pop in the new one (just don't Hulk-smash it). Bayonet bulbs have small prongs; push in slightly, twist to the left, and they'll come free. For specialty bulbs (such as those in ovens or microwaves), check the package for instructions. Sometimes, you need to remove a cover panel with a screwdriver first. ***Always switch off the power before poking around with your hands.*** If a bulb blows repeatedly, that's probably an electrical issue. Call for help rather than risking your eyebrows.

For smoke and carbon monoxide detectors, open the battery compartment (usually located on the back or side), replace the battery (a 9-volt battery is most common), and then hold the test button until it beeps. If it chirps at 3 a.m., it's not haunted; it just wants fresh batteries.

Changing the furnace or A/C filters is a classic "adulting" moment. Filters vary by size and type (check the sticker on your old one or the manual taped inside your closet door). Slide out the old filter—note which way the arrows point—and insert the new one with arrows facing the same way. Do this every three months—or sooner, if you have pets or allergies. You'll breathe easier and might even save on your electric bill.

Clogged Drains and Leaky Faucets

Drains are notorious for clogging at the most inconvenient times. When water won't go down, don't panic. For bathroom sinks or showers, start by pulling out any visible hair or gunk with gloved fingers (gross but effective). Still slow? Try a zip-it tool, a cheap plastic stick with barbs that grabs hidden clogs. For stubborn blockages, pour a half-cup of baking soda followed by a half-cup of vinegar down the drain. Cover the drain with a damp cloth, wait ten minutes, and then flush with hot water. If you hear gurgling or smell a swampy odor after all this, you might need to escalate the issue. Grease clogs in kitchen sinks respond best if you flush them with boiling water after scraping out as much fat as possible with paper towels (though you should never pour grease down the drain in the first place; your pipes will hate you forever). Plungers aren't just for toilets—a few firm plunges can clear minor blockages in sinks as well.

Leaky faucets are like background noise in old apartments, but that drip-drip-drip will drive you up the wall and rack up your water bill. First step: Turn off the water supply under the sink (look for two little valves and turn them clockwise). Plug the drain so nothing small escapes into pipe oblivion. Use an adjustable wrench to unscrew the nut under the handle, wrapping it in a rag first to prevent scratching. Remove the handle and fish out the rubber washer or O-ring inside— these are usually the culprits. Take them to the hardware store for exact replacements (they cost less than a latte). Reverse your steps to put everything back together. Turn on the water slowly and check for leaks. If it's still dripping after you've swapped washers, you might have bigger problems behind the wall. At that point, call maintenance or a plumber.

Fixing Doors and Handles

Doors and windows love to misbehave after a season of humidity or one too many slams. Squeaky hinges? A squirt of WD-40 or even cooking oil will silence them (wipe away any drips so you don't attract dust). If your door doesn't close correctly, check for loose screws on the hinges and tighten them using your screwdriver set. Misaligned doors sometimes need you to back out each screw just enough to shift things, then tighten back up until they close smoothly again. Cabinet handles and drawer pulls like to wiggle loose; you can tighten them with a Phillips screwdriver until snug.

Now, here's where to draw your DIY line: If you ever spot sparks, smell gas, see water pouring from pipes behind walls, or find mystery puddles growing under appliances, put down your tools and back away slowly. Electrical repairs are not worth risking your health (or your eyebrows). Gas leaks require immediate attention from your landlord or the utility company. ***Do not wait or attempt to fix it yourself.*** If water is leaking so badly that towels can't contain it, shut off the main valve if you know where it is, then call maintenance or a professional before the ceilings collapse or mold starts growing.

Fixing stuff yourself feels empowering—and sometimes even fun—but knowing when to call for backup is just as important. You don't have to become Bob Vila overnight. The key is building confidence one minor repair at a time and recognizing when safety comes first.

Basic Laundry Skills—Sorting, Washing, Drying, and Folding

Laundry tends to freak people out for one reason: Nobody wants to end up with baby-sized sweaters or a collection of pink socks when they started with white. The first time I did laundry on my own, I stared at the machine like it might bite. But if you break it down, laundry is like learning to ride a bike. There are wobbly starts, but once you've practiced a few times, you'll wonder why you ever found it intimidating.

First up: decoding those cryptic laundry labels. You know, the ones with hieroglyphics that look straight out of an escape room puzzle? They actually tell you how to avoid disaster. Here's the cheat sheet: A tub with water means machine washable, a triangle signals the use of bleach, a square with a circle indicates tumble drying, and an iron icon is—shocker—about ironing. If the symbol has an X through it, don't do that thing! For example, "Do Not Bleach" (or a bottle with an X over it) means your dark jeans stay dark and don't morph into accidental acid wash. When in doubt, Google the symbol or check the tag's fine print for words you recognize.

Sorting is where laundry victories begin. Dumping everything in at once is tempting (and sometimes hilarious), but separating colors prevents that classic "why is everything blue?" moment. Separate lights (white tees, pale undies), darks (navy, black, deep reds), and brights (neon gym shorts, wild socks). Delicates—anything lacy, slinky, or fancy—get their own pile. Towels and sheets fall into the "heavier stuff" category; they can withstand hotter water and rougher cycles. If you're feeling fancy or have the space, consider separating your workout gear (synthetics) since they dry quickly and can pick up unpleasant smells if washed with everything else. For that first run-through, keep new clothes away from whites; dyes love to bleed when you're not watching.

The sorting chart goes like this:

- **Lights:** whites, beiges, pastels
- **Darks:** black, navy, deep colors
- **Delicates:** bras, lingerie, athletic wear
- **Towels/linens:** bath towels, washcloths, sheets

Let's move to the washing machine itself. If you're staring at a front-loader and wondering where everything goes—relax. Open the door (or lid), toss clothes loosely inside (don't cram them in like clowns in a car). If you fill it up too full, nothing gets truly clean. Next up: detergent. Most loads require about two tablespoons of soap; use even less if you're using high-efficiency (HE) detergent in an HE machine (look for the swirly logo on the door). Overusing detergent can make clothes stiff and trap gunk inside the machine, a common rookie mistake. Pods are easy, but don't toss them on top of dry clothes; throw them in first so the water hits them right away.

Cycle selection sounds trickier than it is. "Normal" or "regular" covers most stuff, including cotton tees, jeans, and pajamas. "Delicate" or "gentle" cycles are best for lace, silk, or workout gear. "Heavy duty" is for towels and sheets. Water temperature can make or break your wardrobe: Cold preserves colors and saves energy, warm works well for everyday grime, and hot is best for white towels or filthy socks. HE machines save water and energy and require less soap.

Regular top-loaders are more forgiving, but they use more water and require careful measuring.

After the wash cycle is complete, you have several options to choose from. Tumble drying is the default for most stuff. If you prefer soft towels and wrinkle-free shirts, opt for "tumble dry low" or "medium." High heat is suitable for sturdy items, such as towels or old jeans, but can quickly shrink or damage delicate fabrics. Clothes likely to shrink (100% cotton tees or anything labeled "pre-shrunk," which is a lie) should air dry on a rack or hanger. This technique extends their life-span and keeps colors from fading. Air-drying delicates prevents weird, misshapen straps or stretched-out elastic.

Folding deserves its own award for being both oddly satisfying and the biggest procrastination magnet ever invented. T-shirts are easy: Turn upside-down, fold the sleeves back, then fold the shirt in thirds lengthwise and again from the bottom up. Pants get folded in half at the knees, then again, so they fit on a shelf or drawer. The fitted sheet —a nemesis for many—has a secret method: Tuck one corner into another until you've got a rough rectangle, then fold as usual. It won't be perfect, but once it's shoved into your closet, nobody will judge. Rolling clothes saves space and keeps wrinkles at bay if you're short on storage space.

Laundry hacks can totally upgrade your routine. Stains are less scary if you act fast. Dab (don't rub!) coffee spills with cold water and soap right away; ink needs hairspray or rubbing alcohol before washing; and grease loves dish soap rubbed gently into the spot before throwing it in the machine. Mesh bags are your best friends: Toss socks or delicates inside so they don't wander off into the mysterious dryer void (and they always do). If you want bonus points for efficiency (and not losing your favorite pair of socks), keep a mesh bag on your hamper and drop socks straight in after wearing them.

Dryer sheets reduce static, but they aren't for everyone. Some people find them irritating or unnecessary if their clothes are air-dried. Wool dryer balls are reusable and help clothes dry faster, eliminating the need for perfumes or chemicals. To avoid shrinking disasters, always double-check labels before tossing anything in high heat.

Forgetful about laundry day? Set reminders on your phone or tie it to another habit (e.g., every Sunday night after dinner). That way, you never have to do a desperate sniff test before work or class again.

Laundry might seem boring until you realize clean clothes boost confidence and help you avoid awkward moments in public. Once these basics become routine, you'll barely think about them, except when teaching a future roommate how not to dye all their underwear pink.

Renters' Rights, Insurance Basics, and When to Call for Help

If you're renting for the first time, it's easy to feel powerless, but you actually have important rights and responsibilities, and knowing them will save you money, stress, and unnecessary parental SOS calls. Maintenance is a two-way street: Your landlord is legally obligated to keep your place safe and livable, which means fixing essentials like heat, water, and appliances. If something significant breaks, such as losing heat in winter, contact your landlord in writing immediately. A quick text works for small issues, but always follow up with an email that includes the date, issue description, and a reasonable repair request deadline. If you get no response, keep a log of your communication. If escalation is needed after several days (usually three or more), check your local laws: You might be able to contact city inspectors or withhold rent until the repairs are made. A clear, documented paper trail generally gets faster results.

Normal wear and tear—like faded paint, carpet worn from pacing during finals, or light scuffs from moving furniture—is not your financial responsibility. However, damage from carelessness (like holes in walls or party stains) is. The difference matters most for your security deposit. When you move in, take date-stamped photos of every room, including walls, floors, appliances, and even hidden spots. Archive these carefully; they're your best defense if the landlord claims damage that was already there on move-out day.

Renters' insurance may sound unnecessary, but it is truly a lifesaver. Imagine a neighbor's kitchen fire damages your stuff, or your laptop gets stolen. Renters insurance generally covers theft, fire, and water damage (excluding flooding, which requires additional coverage), as well as temporary housing if your unit becomes uninhabitable. The average policy costs about $15–25 per month, which is a small investment for significant peace of mind. If you can bundle it with your car insurance, it might cost even less. Shopping for insurance is simple: Compare quotes online, look for strong personal property coverage, and check liability protection in case someone gets hurt in your apartment. List valuable items as required and accurately estimate their replacement costs. Some landlords could require proof of renters' insurance before handing over the keys.

Communicating with landlords or property managers can feel awkward, but you need to be clear and polite and keep conversations in writing whenever possible. For maintenance, a straightforward email is best: "Hi [Landlord], I wanted to let you know our heater stopped working last night (January 10). The apartment is freezing. Could we please have someone come take a look as soon as possible? Thank you!" If noise from neighbors is a problem, document dates and times first, then ask your landlord for help. Always save copies of every exchange—including screenshots—and note when repairs are completed or scheduled. If you need to break a lease, review your contract's early termination clauses and fees. Notify your landlord with a written explanation instead of disappearing.

When landlords ignore repair requests, escalate the process step by step: Send a follow-up message referencing your earlier request, attach photos showing the worsening conditions, and patiently wait for the locally required time (usually 3–7 days). If you still haven't received help, consider checking the tenant advocacy groups, city housing offices, or free mediation services that many cities offer.

Not every household issue is safe or sensible to tackle yourself. Some situations require immediate, professional help. Gas smells? Leave immediately and call the utility company. *Never* attempt to investigate or fix the issue yourself. For water leaks or floods, shut off the main valve (if possible) and contact maintenance immediately. Power outages lasting longer than a brief flicker mean it's time to contact your landlord or the electric company, not fiddle with outlets. If you lose heat or AC during harsh weather, report it right away and find a safe temporary place to stay if needed. Electrical issues, such as sparking outlets or burning smells, should always be left to professionals.

Living on your own means knowing when to handle basics and when to call for help. Knowing your rights shields your deposit and peace of mind. Renters insurance turns potential financial disasters into minor setbacks. Good communication prevents little problems from growing. Spotting genuine emergencies and getting help before things escalate is a true sign of real adulthood.

Mastering these basics lets you thrive, not just survive, in your home. With systems for staying clean, fixing what you can, and managing emergencies, you're ready for anything. Next up: health and wellness —because a tidy home only matters if you feel your best living in it.

Quiz:

1) Which of the following tasks should be done daily to maintain a clean living space?

   A. Washing windows
   B. Deep-cleaning the bathroom
   C. Wiping kitchen counters and doing dishes
   D. Changing HVAC filters

Answer: C

Daily tasks like wiping counters and doing dishes help prevent smells, pests, and mess from building up.

* * *

2) What is a zip-it tool used for?

   A. Fixing zippers on jackets
   B. Catching rodents
   C. Unclogging drains by grabbing hair and gunk
   D. Repairing broken sink handles

Answer: C

A zip-it tool is a plastic strip with barbs that helps remove clogs from bathroom drains.

* * *

3) What's the correct way to treat a laundry stain like grease or ink?

    A. Toss it directly into the dryer
    B. Let it air dry and wash later
    C. Rub it vigorously with hot water
    D. Pretreat with dish soap or rubbing alcohol, then wash

Answer: D

Pretreating stains with the right substance—like dish soap for grease or rubbing alcohol for ink—helps remove them before washing.

4) Why should you take dated photos when you move into a rental?

    A. To decorate later
    B. To compare before and after cleaning
    C. To prove what damage existed before move-in
    D. To help you remember the layout

Answer: C

Dated photos document the rental's original condition, protecting your security deposit from unfair charges.

5) Which situation should prompt you to call a professional immediately?

A. A dripping faucet
B. A squeaky door
C. A lost sock
D. The smell of gas in your apartment

Answer: D

A gas smell could indicate a dangerous leak—leave immediately and call the utility company. Never try to fix it yourself.

* * *

Chapter 7

Health, Wellness, and Self-Care

Scheduling Doctor Visits, Dental Care, and Preventive Health

We've all been there. We've all gotten that "Annual Checkup Overdue!" message at one time or another. Scheduling doctor visits can feel like assembling furniture with missing screws. But healthcare admin is just a series of doable steps, even if you still Google "what counts as a fever" every flu season.

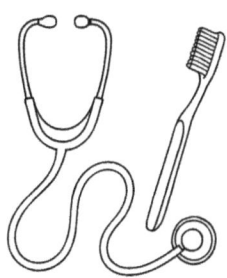

Let's debunk this myth: Finding a primary care doctor or dentist doesn't require special connections. Start with your health insurance card; usually, there's a website or customer service number on the back. Call and ask for names or go online, enter your zip code, and filter for "in-network" providers to avoid surprise bills. No insurance? Many clinics offer sliding-scale fees or student discounts. Friends, family, or your current provider can also recommend trustworthy options. For search terms, try "family medicine," "internal medicine," or "general dentistry."

When contacting a new office, keep it straightforward: "Hi, I'm a new patient and want to schedule a checkup. Do you accept my insurance?" Have your insurance card handy; they'll ask for your member ID and group number. Record your appointment details and any instructions (like fasting before labs). If you're anxious, write out what you want to say; receptionists have heard every kind of question, including, "What do I do if my tooth just fell out?"

A quick insurance primer: Copays, such as $20 for a doctor's visit or $10 for a prescription, are fixed amounts. "In-network" means your provider agrees to your insurer's rates (resulting in lower costs for you); "out-of-network" often means higher costs and more paperwork. Always confirm your provider is in-network before booking more than a checkup.

Scheduling Regular Medical Care

What should you get checked? Young adults typically need an annual physical (even if they're healthy), a dental cleaning every six months (flossing just before your appointment won't fool anyone), and a vision exam every couple of years unless they wear glasses or have vision problems (in which case they should go annually). Get regular STI screenings if you're sexually active. Keep vaccines current: Receive flu shots annually, COVID-19 boosters if recommended, and check for tetanus and HPV updates. Ask your doctor if you need others based on your life or travel plans.

To prep for appointments, bring your insurance card, photo ID, a list of medications (including over-the-counter medicines and vitamins), and a list of allergies. Know your family medical history, if possible. Any instances of diabetes, heart disease, or mental illness? Write down questions or symptoms because it's easy to forget under pressure. Sample questions include, "What screenings do I need at my age?" or "Should I worry about this cough that's lasted two weeks?" Be honest; doctors have seen it all.

Describing symptoms doesn't have to feel awkward. Explain what's happening, when it started, how often, and what affects it. If it's something sensitive, acknowledge your embarrassment briefly. Your provider will appreciate your honesty.

After visits, don't disappear. Ask for test results and visit summaries. Get the patient portal app, if available. It lets you schedule visits, see results, message your providers, and organize your health info. Or keep a simple health folder with lab results, prescriptions, appointment cards, and reminders for future care.

Your Health Admin Power-Up

- **Add appointments and reminders to your phone calendar.**
- **Call and schedule your annual physical and dental cleaning (script it out, if needed).**
- **Find and read your insurance card.**
- **Locate in-network doctors and dentists using your insurer's website.**
- **Prepare a list of all medications and allergies before your visit.**
- **Save visit summaries or test results (digitally or in a folder).**
- **Set reminders to schedule your next checkup or cleaning.**

- **Write down at least two questions per appointment.**

There's no award for avoiding the doctor or trying to substitute mints for brushing. Preventive care might sound dull, but it prevents major issues later. You're doing a good job handling this adulting thing, even if you occasionally misplace your insurance card.

Managing Stress and Anxiety–Grounding Techniques that Work

Stress and anxiety are like those annoying pop-up ads that never really go away. You think you've closed them, but they sneak back when you're least ready, like right before a big presentation or in the middle of the night. Don't freak out, though. Feeling stressed is normal during significant life changes, and honestly, adulthood is just a rolling series of plot twists. Stress isn't just in your head, either. It can feel like a knot in your stomach, sweaty palms, your heart drumming like it's late for class, or a sudden urge to snap at your roommate for breathing too loudly. This is your body's "fight-or-flight" alarm system kicking in. What was useful for running from bears in our cave dwellings now just makes you forget passwords and lose your phone—you know, the one you're holding in your hand.

The 5-4-3-2-1 Method

But you don't have to let stress run the show. Grounding techniques can snap you back into reality faster than a cold shower. One tried-and-true exercise is the 5-4-3-2-1 method: Look around and name five things you can see (the weird stain on the carpet counts), four things you can touch (your jeans, a pencil, maybe your phone), three things you hear (the hum of the fridge, birds, maybe your own impatient sigh), two things you smell (coffee, laundry detergent), and one thing you taste (even if it's just your toothpaste). This hack anchors you in the present moment and slows the hamster wheel in your brain.

The Box-Breathing Method

Box breathing comes in handy when your thoughts are racing. Breathe in for four counts, hold for four, exhale for four, and hold again for four. Repeat a few times, and you might notice your muscles untangling and your mind clearing up, much like a fog lifting after a storm. There's also the "name three things" trick—just pause and mentally list three objects or sounds around you. It's simple but surprisingly effective at shifting your focus away from spiraling worries.

Building a personal stress toolkit involves experimenting with various strategies and collecting those that work for you. Maybe stretching every morning helps, or perhaps taking a quick walk after doom-scrolling on TikTok serves as your reset button. Some people swear by fidget toys or squeezing a stress ball; others need a playlist of calming music or a whiff of their favorite scented lotion to chill out. Don't be afraid to mix things up until you find a combo that feels right. After all, what works for your roommate might not work for you, and that's cool.

Knowing When to Reach Out

It's also smart to know when stress crosses the line into something more significant. Watch for signs like not sleeping (or sleeping way too much), wild mood swings, losing interest in stuff that usually excites you, or pulling away from friends. If daily life feels like you're slogging through mud or if anxiety is your new sidekick 24/7, it's time to reach out. There's no gold star for toughing it out alone.

Talking to a therapist doesn't mean you've failed at adulting; it means you're pretty smart about taking care of yourself. Therapy is just like getting help fixing a flat tire; no one expects you to do it solo. If you're unsure where to start, consider visiting campus health centers and counseling offices or using telehealth apps that connect you with mental health professionals from anywhere with an internet connection. Crisis hotlines are also there for those "I need help now" moments.

If telling someone you're struggling gives you heartburn, use a simple script: "Hey, I've been feeling off lately and could use someone to talk to." You don't have to spill everything at once—just opening the door is enough. When meeting with a counselor or a therapist, it's okay to ask questions like, "What does a session look like?" or "Can we work at my pace?" You deserve support that actually feels supportive.

Stress doesn't vanish overnight, but learning what calms you puts power back in your hands. Try stuff out. Keep what helps. Share with friends who are on the same emotional rollercoaster. Taking care of your mind is just as important as looking after your body—and way less complicated than figuring out taxes.

Building a Basic First Aid Kit and Handling Minor Emergencies

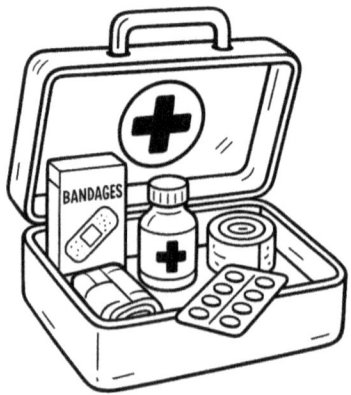

There's nothing quite like realizing you need a bandage and discovering your only options are a wrinkled fast-food napkin and some duct tape. Every adult should have at least one solid first aid kit, and no, the bag of cough drops rattling around in your backpack does not count. You don't need a fancy, hospital-grade setup, just a kit stocked for the sort of "oops" moments that happen between classes, at work, or when you accidentally attempt to slice an avocado and get your hand instead. Start simple and cheap: Grab assorted bandages (the regular strips, plus a few big ones for actual "oh no" moments), antibiotic ointment to stop those scrapes from getting gross, tweezers (because splinters have no chill), alcohol wipes to clean up cuts, basic pain relievers such as acetaminophen or ibuprofen, some allergy meds for those mystery sneezes or rashes, and an instant cold pack for bumps and bruises. If you want to feel super prepared, toss in gauze pads and a roll of medical tape, but don't stress if you skip the more advanced items at first.

Knowing what to do with all this is half the battle. First things first: With minor cuts or scrapes, start by washing your hands (germs are not your friends). Use an alcohol wipe or rinse the wound with clean water—don't pour on hydrogen peroxide unless you want a chemistry class re-enactment on your skin. Dab dry with a clean tissue. Apply a little antibiotic ointment and cover with a bandage. Change it daily, or if it gets wet or dirty. For burns from your latest kitchen experiment gone wrong, run cool (not icy) water over the burn for several minutes. Don't pop blisters, even if they look super tempting. Let them heal under a clean bandage. Minor scrapes deserve the same treatment: clean, apply ointment, cover, and carry on.

Splinters are tiny jerks. Clean the area first, then use your tweezers (sterilize them with alcohol) to grab the splinter as close to the skin as possible and pull it straight out—no twisting. If part remains or it's really deep, don't dig around; sometimes you need a pro to finish the job. Wash the area and throw on a bandage if it bleeds.

There might be times when you hit situations too big for your kit. If bleeding is heavy and won't stop after ten minutes of direct pressure, if someone faints and doesn't wake up fast, if there's difficulty breathing, severe burns, a head injury with confusion or vomiting, or any sign of infection (like redness, swelling, pus, or fever), call for help immediately. Urgent care is suitable for conditions such as deep cuts that might require stitches or burns larger than the size of your palm. Call 911 for anything life-threatening or if you're unsure and things appear genuinely alarming.

Keeping your kit stocked is a valuable life skill in itself. Place it somewhere obvious—bathroom cabinets work well at home, desk drawers are great for dorms, and backpack versions are handy for the accident-prone (no shame). Every few months, or at the start of each semester, check expiration dates on ointments and meds. Expired stuff won't help much when you actually need it. Restock what you've used so that next time, you're not improvising with paper towels and hope.

Your No-Nonsense First Aid Kit

- **Alcohol wipes**
- **Allergy medication**
- **Antibiotic ointment**
- **Assorted bandages (small and large)**
- **Gauze pads and tape (bonus points)**
- **Instant cold pack**
- **Pain reliever (acetaminophen/ibuprofen)**
- **Tweezers**

Having this kit ready means that the next time you take a tumble or try to be a kitchen superhero, you can patch yourself up without panic—or duct tape.

Sleep Hygiene—Real Strategies for Restful Nights

Sleep is like Wi-Fi for your brain: When it's strong, everything works better; when it's weak, everything lags. After a rough night spent tossing, turning, or scrolling social media, you know the aftermath—groggy mornings, forgetfulness, zoning out, and general irritability. Exhaustion tanks your mood, saps focus, and leaves you unsure if you did that important thing or just dreamt about it. Without good sleep, even your wittiest jokes fall flat. In addition, chronic, inadequate sleep harms your immune system, memory, appetite, and even your skin. Sleep is the underlying ingredient that keeps your entire system running, and missing out on it will cause everything to break down eventually.

A Sleep-Friendly Environment

Creating a sleep-friendly environment doesn't require a fancy spa vibe or an outrageously priced mattress. Start with managing light, as your body takes darkness as a cue to sleep. Use blackout curtains if artificial light sneaks into your room, or try a cheap sleep mask if your roommate loves their night light or the sun rises too early for your liking. Noise is another sleep disruptor. If your place is loud—whether due to traffic, animals, or chatty neighbors—try using a white noise machine or app, running a fan, or wearing earplugs. The bottom line is consistency, with regular signals helping your brain wind down.

A Sleep-Friendly Routine

Routines at night are important, and they should be more effective than scrolling through your phone until it slips out of your hands. Rituals signal your body that it's time to relax. Choose something screen-free: Read a real book (those with pages) or do some gentle stretching to release tension—just five minutes helps. For over-thinkers replaying the day's awkward moments or old worries, try keeping a notebook by your bed for a "brain dump." Write down thoughts and tasks so they don't keep spinning in your mind. If you want to cultivate a positive habit, jot down three things you're grateful for each day; it's a great way to steer clear of stress and focus on what's going well.

Roommates are a classic challenge because rarely do sleep schedules match. If your roommate is up watching movies or having late-night debates, discuss respectful "quiet hours" or invest in an eye mask and noise-canceling headphones. If friendly negotiation fails, you can always joke about sticky note diplomacy. Odd schedules—late shifts, early classes, unexpected adventures—also can throw your sleep off. To cope, anchor at least one part of your day: Wake up at the same time or maintain a particular bedtime ritual, regardless of when you turn in.

Phones are a major sleep saboteur. If you let yourself keep scrolling, you'll lose hours before you notice. Set your phone to "do not disturb" at night, turn off unnecessary notifications, and move it out of reach— this keeps you from checking the time too often. If you need an alarm, consider a basic clock instead of your phone. If you're lying awake after a tough day, don't force sleep. Get up, do something low-key and boring (like folding socks), then try sleeping again once you're calmer.

Sleep hygiene requires simple, consistent changes. Upgrade an uncomfortable mattress or itchy sheets when you can, but focus on the basics first. Test different combinations to see what works: an eye mask paired with mellow music, a book with stretching, or simply darkness and quiet. Don't treat sleep as an afterthought, as it's essential maintenance for your brain and mood. Even small efforts add up, making it easier to wake up clear-headed and ready for the day, even if "ready" means pouring your coffee without spilling it.

Self-Care Routines on a Budget—What Matters Most

Let's get this straight: Self-care isn't just some influencer's excuse to buy overpriced candles and post about it with a #Blessed caption. Authentic self-care is essential maintenance for your brain and body, not a luxury reserved for those with time, money, or a bathtub that doesn't also serve as a laundry rack. If you've ever wondered whether you're "doing it right" because you're not sipping green juice in Bali, relax. The truth? Self-care is less about indulgence and more about not running yourself into the ground.

What counts as self-care? For most people, it's the unsung, ordinary things that keep their stress levels from going nuclear. Step outside for a quick walk—fresh air does more than chill your phone. Listen to your favorite playlist and dance like nobody's watching (or, for bonus points, do it in your socks, sliding across the kitchen floor). Grab a notebook and jot down whatever's on your mind. It doesn't have to be profound; just get it out. Call or text someone who genuinely cares, even if all you say is, "Hey, my brain feels scrambled." You can even turn your bathroom into a spa with a hot shower, some lotion, and five minutes of deep breathing. None of this needs to cost more than a bus fare or a cheap cup of coffee.

The trick is figuring out what helps you recharge. Not everyone vibes with yoga or meditation, and running might cause you to break out in hives (mentally or physically). That's fine! Try out different routines and notice how you feel before and after each one. Maybe you keep a sticky note on your desk: "Mood before: 4/10. Mood after the walk: 7/10." Or throw a "reset day" on the calendar after an exhausting week, when you can eat breakfast at noon and ignore everyone for a few hours. Weekdays might call for quick fixes, such as stretching between Zoom calls, while weekends allow you to go all-in with hobbies or take longer walks somewhere quiet and green.

Don't get caught up chasing the latest "self-care must-have" trending online. Social media often presents everything in a visually appealing and expensive light, so don't fall for it. If unplugging from Instagram for an evening makes you feel more human, that counts as self-care, too. Comparing your downtime to someone else's highlight reel is the opposite of helpful. Focus on what actually leaves you feeling less frazzled, not what racks up views.

Excuses pop up faster than pimples before prom. Perhaps you dislike exercise, or the weather outside is giving its best "apocalypse" impression. No gym? No problem. Try chair workouts, YouTube yoga in your bedroom, or pace around during phone calls—movement is movement. If motivation is low, aim for something tiny: fifteen jumping jacks, five minutes cleaning, or pulling out paints you haven't touched since middle school. Celebrate the small wins—did you laugh at a meme today? Did you remember to eat lunch? These are victories, too.

Remember, self-care isn't about hitting some mythical wellness quota. It's about staying functional and feeling decent most of the time. You're not looking for perfect. Experiment with what works for you and adjust things as seasons change or your schedule shifts. The main thing is showing up for yourself, even if that means putting on clean socks or saying "nope" to one more obligation.

As you work through these routines, keep it real and make it yours. Nobody else gets to define what refuels you but you. Sometimes, it's a walk; sometimes, it's binge-watching cartoons while eating cereal straight from the box. Either way, if it leaves you feeling better, it counts.

Try This: Mini–Mood Tracker

Each day this week, scribble down one thing you did just for yourself and rate your mood before and after. Over time, patterns emerge, so use them to build a personal self-care menu that works for you.

When you treat self-care as regular upkeep instead of some rare treat, everything else starts to fall into place more easily, including energy, mood, and all those other life skills you're building. Up next: Let's explore how these healthy habits relate to professional life and advancing at work or school.

Quiz:

1) What should you bring to a doctor's appointment?

   A. A toothbrush and toothpaste
   B. A list of your favorite foods
   C. Your insurance card, photo ID, and list of medications/allergies
   D. Nothing—it's all in their system

Answer: C

Always bring your insurance card, photo ID, and a list of medications and allergies to ensure accurate care and avoid confusion.

* * *

2) Which grounding technique uses your senses to calm anxiety?

   A. The caffeine challenge
   B. 5-4-3-2-1 method
   C. Flash card memorization
   D. Sleep deprivation reset

Answer: B

The 5-4-3-2-1 technique uses sight, touch, hearing, smell, and taste to bring your mind back to the present during anxiety.

* * *

3) Which item is NOT typically found in a basic first aid kit?

   A. Antibiotic ointment
   B. Gauze pads
   C. Chocolate bars
   D. Tweezers

Answer: C

Chocolate bars might help your mood, but they're not part of a basic first aid kit.

4) What is a good nighttime routine to improve sleep hygiene?

   A. Watching intense action movies
   B. Scrolling through social media until you pass out
   C. Doing gentle stretches and reading a real book
   D. Keeping bright lights on to stay alert

Answer: C

Screen-free activities like light stretching and reading signal the body to wind down for restful sleep.

5) Which of the following does count as real self-care?

   A. Doing a dance break in your kitchen
   B. Comparing your routine to influencers online
   C. Buying expensive spa products only for show
   D. Skipping meals to save time

Answer: A

Self-care is about what genuinely helps you recharge—like moving your body in fun, affordable ways.

* * *

Chapter 8

Career Launch and Professional Skills

Creating a Standout Résumé and Cover Letter

Staring at a blank document to write your résumé can feel overwhelming, but think of your résumé not as a boring list but as your highlight reel, a personal trailer for your next blockbuster role. For first-time job seekers, your résumé is designed to demonstrate your potential, even if your experience comes from part-time jobs, volunteer roles, or extracurricular activities. At the top, lead with your name (in big, bold letters), phone number, professional email address (without silly handles), and city and state. Next, add education details: school, graduation date, and major/minor. If your experience is limited, prioritize education to highlight your strengths.

In your skills section, spotlight relevant abilities, including proficiency in Microsoft Office, basic coding, foreign languages, or social media, depending on the job. Under experience, include all paid, unpaid, or volunteer work. For each role, list your job title, organization, city, and dates. Add 2–4 concise bullet points highlighting your achievements, using action verbs like "organized," "created," or "assisted." If coursework is relevant (such as Intro to Marketing for a social media position), add a "Relevant Coursework" section, and don't forget to include certifications or training (e.g., CPR, Google Analytics, or food safety).

Skip filler sections. Objectives aren't necessary, and hobbies are only worth mentioning if they are directly related. Avoid using fancy fonts, personal photos, and content from before high school. Be honest about your skills. Don't overstate abilities or include things you barely know. Employers want authenticity.

Customize each résumé to the job. Carefully read the job description and extract keywords from the requirements and responsibilities. If the employer is looking for someone with team leadership skills, use language like "led team project in environmental science club." Think creatively about your experience: Babysitting can become "managed scheduling and conflict resolution for multiple clients (ages 2–7)," and organizing fundraisers could be "coordinated events raising $500+ for local causes." Connect your experiences to their needs.

Cover letters are an extra step, but they matter. Don't say, "See attached résumé." Instead, treat your cover letter as a first impression. Address it to a specific person when possible ("Dear Ms. Patel" is better than "To Whom It May Concern"). Open with the job title and a brief, genuine note on why you're interested, and skip clichés. In the body, share a short, specific story about an accomplishment that's relevant to the job—numbers stand out ("increased club attendance by 30%" is better than "improved club participation"). Close by connecting your story to the company's mission or goals, and always thank them for their time.

Formatting counts. Use classic fonts (such as Arial or Calibri) in 11–12-pt size with margins of at least 0.5 inches. Save your résumé as a PDF to preserve formatting. Avoid complicated tables or graphics, so Applicant Tracking Systems don't have trouble reading your résumé. Use clear headings (e.g., "Education" or "Experience"). Proofread carefully, use spell check, and have someone else review your documents for errors.

Sample Résumé Focus

For customer service, emphasize communication ("Assisted 30+ customers daily"), teamwork ("Collaborated with five coworkers to manage operations"), and patience ("Resolved complaints under pressure"). For administrative roles, highlight organization ("Scheduled appointments for three managers"), technology ("Managed office calendar using Google Suite"), and accuracy ("Processed invoices with 99% error-free rate"). Adjust your bullet points to fit the role. Here is an example:

Jordan Taylor

Charlotte, NC • (555) 123-4567 • jordan.taylor@email.com
June 29, 2025

Ms. Asha Patel

Youth Programs Coordinator

Charlotte Community Center

Charlotte, NC

Dear Ms. Patel,

I'm writing to apply for the Summer Youth Program Assistant position at the Charlotte Community Center. As a high school student deeply engaged in volunteer work and youth leadership, I'm excited about the opportunity to contribute to a program that empowers young people in our city.

While serving as a volunteer with the Key Club at Westview High School, I coordinated a school-wide food drive that collected over 1,000 items for local shelters. I also helped organize bake sales that raised over $500 for community causes. Through these efforts, I developed strong skills in event coordination, team collaboration, and community engagement—skills I believe align closely with the goals of your youth programming.

Your mission to provide safe, enriching summer activities for children resonates with my own passion for service and youth development. I would welcome the opportunity to bring my energy, creativity, and organizational skills to your team.

Thank you for considering my application. I look forward to the possibility of contributing to your program and learning from your incredible staff.

Sincerely,

Jordan Taylor

JORDAN TAYLOR

(555) 123-4567 • jordan.taylor@email.com • Charlotte, NC

EDUCATION

Westview High School, Charlotte, NC

Expected Graduation: June 2025

GPA: 3.8 | Honors Student

Relevant Coursework: Intro to Marketing, Digital Media, Public Speaking

SKILLS

- Proficient in Microsoft Word, Excel, and PowerPoint
- Basic HTML & CSS
- Conversational Spanish
- Canva and Instagram for content creation
- Strong written and verbal communication

EXPERIENCE

Fundraising Volunteer

Westview High School Key Club – Charlotte, NC

Sept 2023 – Present

- Coordinated a school-wide food drive, collecting over 1,000 items for local shelters
- Created digital flyers and promoted events through social media
- Assisted in organizing bake sales that raised $500+ for community causes

Babysitter (Freelance)

Private Families – Charlotte, NC

Summer 2022 – Present

- Managed care for children aged 2–7 across three households
- Handled scheduling, conflict resolution, and activity planning
- Ensured safety and engagement through creative games and routines

CERTIFICATIONS

- CPR & First Aid Certified (American Red Cross)
- Food Handler Safety Training (State of North Carolina)

PROJECTS & LEADERSHIP

Environmental Science Club Project Leader

Westview High School

- Led a team of 6 students to plan and execute a recycling awareness campaign
- Organized school cleanup day with over 50 participants

- **Is my entire contact information present, including a professional email?**
- **Is education first if I have limited experience?**
- **Are bullet points specific and action-oriented?**
- **Did I include keywords from the job posting?**
- **Is my cover letter addressed to a real person and shares a brief, relevant story?**
- **Did I proofread at least twice and have someone else check?**
- **Is my document saved as a PDF with my name in the filename?**

Remember, every professional started with a blank page. Keep it concise, tailored, and true to yourself.

LinkedIn and Online Networking—Building Your Digital Brand

Creating a LinkedIn profile is like arriving at a job fair prepared and polished. Use a clear, friendly headshot of yourself (skip the party pics, pets, or blurry selfies), and be intentional with your headline. Move beyond "Student" or "Unemployed" and opt for something like "Aspiring Marketing Coordinator | Social Media Enthusiast | College Grad" or "Entry-Level Data Analyst | Excel Fanatic | Problem Solver." Aim for honesty and specificity; there's no need for grandiose titles.

In the About or Summary section, write a few sentences that explain your interests and what you're looking for. Highlight what you enjoy (e.g., creative storytelling, analyzing data, or organizing events) and sprinkle in a fun fact or two. Let your personality show, but keep it concise.

When listing experience, don't worry if you haven't held a traditional job. Include internships, part-time work, volunteer efforts, or leadership in clubs (such as running social media, tutoring, or coordinating events). Add bullet points that focus on what you accomplished, not just your responsibilities.

Skills and endorsements are like digital "props" from your peers. List everything relevant to your goals—e.g., communication, teamwork, Canva, and Python—and ask classmates or colleagues to endorse you. Education is straightforward: List your school, degree, and dates. If you have certifications (from CPR to Google Analytics or Excel courses), include them.

Online networking requires a standard, friendly approach. Always personalize connection requests: "Hi, I'm a recent grad interested in your field and would love to connect" is much better than the generic invite. Once connected, don't immediately ask for a job. Start with an informational interview or a casual chat to learn more about their career path ("Would you be open to a quick call so I can learn more about your work and how you got started?"). Afterward, thank them and mention something specific you learned from the conversation. People appreciate knowing their help made a difference.

Posting on LinkedIn is like joining a professional party. Don't overshare, but don't be a silent observer, either. Share articles with a quick comment ("Great tips here for new designers—I'm going to try that color palette trick!"), and congratulate connections on promotions or new jobs with a "Congrats!" or short, direct message. Regular engagement helps boost your visibility and helps others think of you when opportunities arise.

Expanding Beyond LinkedIn

Networking isn't limited to LinkedIn. You can connect and grow your brand on platforms such as Twitter/X, Reddit, and Discord. Each space is unique. On Twitter/X, follow industry professionals and occasionally reply to their posts thoughtfully. On Reddit, subreddits like r/jobs or r/careerguidance offer helpful advice, but be mindful of the group rules and refrain from oversharing personal information. On Discord, join servers relevant to your interests, introduce yourself, and join discussions before sharing your work.

Finding industry groups requires some effort, but it's worth it. Look for LinkedIn groups tied to your field or interests and join the conversation—don't stay silent. When you complete a significant project (e.g., organizing an event or developing an app for class), share a short post about your learning experience. If possible, add photos or visuals to help your content stand out.

Ultimately, your digital presence should convey that you're intelligent, motivated, and someone people want to work with. Stay positive and professional, but let your genuine personality come through. The goal isn't to seem perfect but to show you're curious, engaged, and open to learning—exactly what future employers value.

Job Interview Confidence–Common Questions and How to Answer Them

Interviews are like high-stakes first dates, except instead of worrying about your teeth, you're anxious about Wi-Fi glitches or blanking on your own name. Whether it's in-person, by phone, or over Zoom, every interview follows a rhythm. There's always some small talk— about the weather, traffic, or the inevitable "Can you hear me okay?" with virtual meetings. In-person, project confidence with a firm handshake and avoid tripping on the way in. For phone interviews, your voice carries everything—keep water handy and remember to smile (it really does come through). On video calls, set your scene: tidy up your background, check your camera angle, and use good lighting so you don't look ominous.

Then, you'll face the usual batch of questions. "Tell me about yourself" isn't an invitation for your autobiography—give them a highlight reel:

your background, current status ("I just graduated from State College with a biology degree"), and why you're interested in the role ("I want to apply my research skills in a real-world setting"). For "Describe a challenge and how you handled it," skip clichés like "I'm a perfectionist." Select a real-life example, such as a messy group project. Clearly explain what happened, what you did to fix it, and the result ("We divided tasks by strengths and finished on time"). When asked, "Why do you want to work here?" go beyond "I need a job." Point to something specifically appealing about the company or the work.

The STAR Method

The STAR method is your go-to for behavioral questions:

- **Situation:** Briefly set the scene.
- **Task:** What was your responsibility?
- **Action:** What did you do?
- **Result:** What happened?

For instance, if asked about handling conflict: "In my student council position (Situation), we had to plan an event with no budget (Task). I rallied the team, organized brainstorming sessions, and contacted local businesses for donations (Action). We got enough supplies for a successful event (Result)." The STAR structure helps keep answers focused and shows off what you can do.

Nonverbal cues are just as important. Sit straight—good posture says you're attentive. Make eye contact, but don't stare. Nod to show you're engaged. Resist fidgeting or crossing your arms. Shaky hands? Keep them relaxed on your lap or the table. On video, look at the camera to simulate strong eye contact.

Nerves are normal. Practice answers with a friend or in front of a mirror (or your phone, where you can spot habits like repeating "um" or "like"). Before your interview, do some slow breathing—inhale for four counts, hold for four, exhale for four. This simple exercise helps calm nerves.

After the interview, don't just wait anxiously. Send a thank-you email within 24 hours, and keep it short, polite, and specific ("Thank you for meeting with me today. I enjoyed learning about your team's work on Project X and am excited about potentially joining the company"). If you get rejected, ask for feedback if possible ("Thank you for considering me. I'd appreciate any feedback so I can improve"). You might not always get a response, but treat each interview as a learning experience. Mistakes happen, but interviewers have seen it all, and you'll get better with practice.

Workplace Etiquette—From Dress Code to Email Sign-Offs

Getting ready for your first day at work is a wild ride. You stare at your closet, wondering if people still wear ties outside of weddings or if "business casual" means khakis and a tucked-in shirt or just jeans without holes. Dress codes are like secret codes; no one ever hands you the decoder ring for them, so it helps to break them down.

- **Professional** usually means suits, dress shirts or blouses, formal shoes, and maybe even a blazer or tie. You're aiming for "I could appear in a legal drama" energy. For interviews and big meetings, look sharp. Think slacks or a skirt, button-down or blouse, and polished shoes (leave the sneakers and flashy socks for another day).
- **Business casual** dials it down a notch: chinos, dress pants, or a neat skirt, collared shirts, cardigans, and closed-toe shoes. No hoodies or graphic tees here.
- Fridays in some places loosen up with **casual**; clean jeans and simple tops are fair game. Still, avoid anything you'd wear to a cookout or on laundry day. If you're not sure

what's expected, look around on your first day, see what
your boss and colleagues wear, and aim to match their vibe.

Workplace Communication

Workplace communication is a whole different animal from chatting
with your friends. When greeting someone in person, be confident
yet straightforward. "Good morning" with a smile goes further than
you think. If you're meeting someone new, throw in a firm handshake
(not bone-crushing but not limp, either—practice with a friend if you
need to) and say your name clearly. If you forget someone's name five
seconds after they say it, you're not alone. Ask again politely or sneak
a peek at their ID badge, if available. In meetings, stay attentive, nod
along, and leave your phone stashed away. Nothing says "I'm not
listening" like scrolling Instagram while your manager is explaining
next quarter's goals.

Now, let's talk about email, the bread and butter of office communication. Your subject line should be clear—think "Request: Schedule
Change for Friday," not "Hey." Greetings set the tone: "Hi [Name]"
or "Hello [Name]" works every time. Skip "Hey!" unless you know
the person very well. Emojis and slang don't belong in work emails;
save those for your group chat. Write short paragraphs and get right
to the point ("I'm following up on the meeting notes from yesterday"). If you're making a request, spell it out plainly. Never assume
your reader can read your mind through the screen. Sign off with
something neutral but friendly, such as "Best regards," "Sincerely," or
simply "Thanks." Add your name and, if applicable, your job title.
Before hitting send, run spellcheck and give it a quick scan for typos
or accidental "Reply All" disasters.

Punctuality is important because by arriving on time, you're showing
respect for everyone else's schedule. Set calendar reminders for meetings or deadlines; seriously, nothing says unreliable like missing the
Monday-morning Zoom because you forgot to set an alarm. If you're
running late (it happens), send a quick message or call to let people

know as soon as possible. Don't ghost your team; they'll appreciate the heads-up even if you're only five minutes behind. Reliability is about more than time: Follow through on what you say you'll do, whether that's turning in a report or cleaning up after yourself in the break room. When you consistently demonstrate that you can be counted on, coworkers start to trust you with more significant responsibilities (and forgive occasional mistakes).

Attitude is contagious in any environment, but especially at work. You don't have to be the office cheerleader (unless that's your thing), but bring positive energy when possible—offer help when someone looks frazzled, say thank you often, and stay cool when something inevitably goes sideways. People notice who keeps their head when others are losing theirs. If you mess up—and you will—own up to it quickly and fix it, if possible. Nobody expects perfection, but everyone appreciates honesty and effort.

Getting along in any workplace is part science, part art, and a good chunk of luck, but these basics will keep you from accidentally becoming "the person who microwaved fish," or worse, the one everyone dreads getting an email from. Navigating dress codes, greetings, emails, punctuality, and attitude doesn't require superpowers—just attention to detail and a willingness to learn from each day's surprises.

Starting Your First Job—What to Expect and How to Succeed

Starting your first "real" job feels like jumping into a new reality show, complete with endless paperwork and the grand prize: a steady paycheck. Your first day will revolve around HR forms and company policies. You might also get a crash course on benefits you didn't realize existed. Come prepared with a folder containing your ID, Social Security card, direct deposit information, and any other requested documents. Arriving organized shows reliability and that you read the onboarding email, and as an added bonus, you'll be set for direct deposit without last-minute scrambling.

After the paperwork comes a blur of introductions. You'll meet loads of people and forget many names by lunchtime, but that's normal. Prepare a short self-introduction, like: "Hi, I'm Taylor—just graduated from State University, excited to join the team and learn the ropes." This keeps things simple and helps people remember you.

The first week is information overload: training sessions, office tours, and possibly a surprising number of safety videos. To stay organized, take notes on your phone or in a small notebook about names, logins, bathroom locations, and any other helpful information. Memorization isn't expected, but showing you're attentive definitely gets noticed.

Every workplace has unwritten rules—the stuff not covered in handbooks but crucial for fitting in. Observe the rhythm: What time do people start? Are lunch breaks social or solo? Do coworkers eat at their desks or head to the break room? How do meetings work—does everyone speak up or wait for prompts? When in doubt, ask someone approachable about the office norms: "When do most people take lunch?" or "Are there team traditions I should know?" Most will be happy to fill you in on things like avoiding microwaving fish or labeling your food.

Mistakes will happen—sometimes right away, sometimes after your third cup of coffee. What matters is your response. If you slip up, admit it promptly: "I realized I made an error entering that data—how should I fix it?" or "Sorry I missed that deadline; could you share advice for next time?" Acknowledging issues promptly demonstrates maturity and a willingness to improve. Managers prefer employees who ask for help over those who avoid problems until it's too late. Apologize if necessary, correct what you can, and move on.

Don't get stuck just getting through each day. Establish clear personal goals such as enhancing your speed, mastering new software, or contributing to a project outside of your primary role. Volunteer for new opportunities, even if it's just organizing a team lunch or shadowing another department. If you admire someone's work—a supervisor or seasoned coworker—ask if they'd be open to giving advice as you settle in. You don't have to call it "mentoring"; just request their insights.

Growth at work requires building skills and relationships you'll use throughout your career. Stay curious, take initiative, and seek feedback as an opportunity rather than a criticism. Every question you ask, mistake you fix, and goal you pursue builds a foundation for future opportunities.

Everyone feels out of place at first. Be adaptable—observe, ask questions, learn from your mistakes, and seek new challenges. Nail these basics now, and the rest of "adulting" will seem less mysterious. Up next: how emotional intelligence and strong relationships smooth out both your career and your life.

Quiz:

1) Which of the following should NOT be included on your resume?

   A. High school babysitting experience with action verbs
   B. A relevant certification like CPR or Google Analytics
   C. A personal photo or fun font to make it stand out
   D. Volunteer work with specific accomplishments

Answer: C

Resumes should be clean and professional—avoid personal photos, fancy fonts, or anything distracting.

* * *

2) What's a strong way to begin a cover letter?

   A. "To Whom It May Concern, I'm writing to apply for any job you have."
   B. "Hi! My resume is attached. Please read it."
   C. "Dear Ms. Lee, I'm applying for the Social Media Intern role because I enjoy creative storytelling and engaging with online communities."
   D. "Hey there! I'm cool and would be great for this."

Answer: C

A strong opening is tailored, specific, and addressed to a real person when possible.

* * *

3) What is the STAR method used for?

   A. Creating a resume summary
   B. Outlining a thank-you note
   C. Answering behavioral interview questions
   D. Ranking your top job choices

Answer: C

The STAR method helps structure interview answers: Situation, Task, Action, and Result.

* * *

4) Which of the following is a good LinkedIn headline for a student?

   A. "Unemployed but hopeful"
   B. "Aspiring Digital Marketer | Canva Enthusiast | Psychology Grad"
   C. "Just a regular person, figuring it out"
   D. "Looking for work – hire me!"

Answer: B

A headline should be clear, positive, and reflect your skills or career goals.

* * *

5) What's a professional email sign-off?

   A. "Laterz,"
   B. "Peace out,"
   C. "Best regards,"
   D. "Don't forget me!"

Answer: C

Stick with classic, courteous sign-offs like "Best regards," "Sincerely," or "Thanks."

* * *

Chapter 9

Communication, Relationships, and Emotional Intelligence

Active Listening and Assertive Communication— Getting Your Point Across

Ever talk to someone and realize they're just waiting for their turn to speak, not actually listening? Maybe you're sharing your chaotic day—spilled coffee, missed bus, epic paper jam—and their response is, "That reminds me of the time..." This is classic passive listening: They're physically present but mentally elsewhere. In contrast, active listening is a crucial skill. It means giving someone your undivided attention—no secret texting or zoning out. You're not just hearing words but also understanding their feelings and intent. Engaged listeners build stronger relationships and help others feel valued and understood.

So, how do you practice active listening without feeling awkward or robotic? Start by putting down your phone. Nothing kills a conversation faster than scrolling while someone's opening up. Make casual eye contact (not a staring contest), nod occasionally, and respond thoughtfully instead of just waiting for your turn to talk. Ask questions if something isn't clear ("Can you tell me more about that?")

and recap what you've heard ("It sounds like you felt overwhelmed when your group ditched you?"). This makes people feel heard. Resist the urge to interrupt, even if you're itching to share your story. If your mind wanders, simply bring it back, which becomes easier with practice, I promise.

When it comes to expressing yourself, assertive communication is key. It's the balance between staying silent and coming on too strong. Assertiveness means stating your needs and opinions clearly but respectfully, without drama or apologizing for how you feel. Use "I" statements—e.g., "I feel frustrated when the dishes pile up because I like a clean space." That's more effective (and less likely to cause a fight) than "You never clean up!" It makes the person you are talking to feel less defensive because you are saying how you feel, not how they make you feel. For saying no, keep it direct but polite—e.g., "I can't pick up your shift Friday, but I hope you find someone." Show empathy and acknowledge the other person's feelings even as you explain your view.

Practice Time: Real-World Communication Scenarios

Try these real-life scripts:

- **Roommate blasting music? "Hey, I'm trying to study, and it's a bit loud. Can we turn it down for an hour?"**
- **Need feedback at work? "I'd appreciate any tips on how I can improve my last project."**
- **Group project slacker? "I noticed I've been doing most of the work. Can we split tasks more evenly?"**
- **Feeling drained? "I'm wiped out and need some solo time tonight. Can we catch up tomorrow?"**

Role-play these with a friend. The more you practice assertive language and active listening, the easier it is

to handle tough conversations with less stress and more confidence.

Mastering the Art of the "Clapback" (Without Drama)

Everyone's seen a "clapback"—that quick-witted response when someone throws shade or makes a joke at your expense. While firing back can be satisfying, it's easy to cross the line from defending yourself to starting unnecessary drama. A true clapback is self-defense with finesse; it's setting boundaries while keeping the atmosphere chill and avoiding unnecessary conflict. If you're always eager for a comeback, pause and consider: *Is this worth my energy, or am I just fueling drama?* Sometimes, silence is more powerful, especially when someone is just fishing for a reaction.

Learning when to respond and when to let things go takes practice. If teasing turns disrespectful, you have every right to speak up. However, if it's friendly banter, it's best to shrug it off. When you do choose to respond, remain calm and avoid personal attacks. Think of crafting your response as if you were adding just enough spice to a recipe: Make your point without ruining the vibe for everyone. Humor is your best tool; a playful, well-timed line can shut down rude comments without making them awkward. If someone says, "Wow, you're actually on time," a reply like, "Miracles do happen—should've bought a lottery ticket" gets your point across without drama. Simple one-liners, such as "Thanks for the feedback. I'll add it to my collection" or "I see we're doing sarcasm today. Good to know," can easily defuse tension.

Before responding, take a moment to check in with yourself. Are you genuinely upset or just surprised? Strong emotions can cloud your judgment, leading to regrets. Take a few breaths before you reply. Ask yourself if you'd say the same thing in front of someone you respect, like your grandma, professor, or future boss. If not, consider rephrasing or staying quiet. If things get heated, give yourself time to cool off: Take a walk, vent to a friend, or write out your thoughts (and then maybe delete them).

Practicing helps. Role-play annoying situations with a friend—for example, someone making fun of your outfit or critiquing your work—and test out different responses. Notice which makes you feel confident but not cruel.

Humor often works wonders: "Guess I missed the dress code. Next time, I'll wear my superhero cape." At other times, keep it short and factual: "I'm good with my choices, thanks." You don't need to win every exchange. The real win is keeping your composure and knowing when to disengage rather than amplifying conflicts that aren't worth your time.

Managing Roommate, Friend, and Family Conflicts

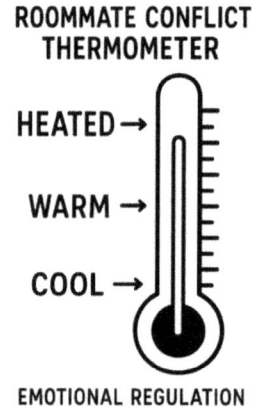

Conflict is as natural in relationships as dust bunnies under the bed—no matter how tidy you think things are, eventually, something pops up. If you haven't argued over whose turn it is to take out the trash or groaned about a mystery guest gobbling your leftovers, just wait. Messy kitchens, unpaid bills, thumping bass late at night, and surprise sleepovers tend to become sparks for arguments. When I moved in with roommates, we hit our first snag over dirty dishes. One person thought "I'll get it tomorrow" was a perfectly reasonable plan, while the rest of us started fantasizing about paper plates as a way of life. Tension grew until someone snapped, and a full-on dish debate broke out in the group chat. If this sounds familiar, congratulations! You're officially living with humans.

Instead of pretending everything's fine or stuffing your feelings until you explode, there's a way to tackle conflict without turning your living space into a reality TV episode. Before you do anything else, cool off. Take a walk, listen to angry music, or write an angry note (but don't deliver it). Set a time to talk so nobody's ambushed when they're hangry or mid–binge watch. When everyone sits down together, remain calm and avoid using accusatory language. Start with facts—"I noticed the kitchen's been messy all week"— instead of "You never clean up!" That switch keeps people from going on the defensive faster than you can say, "passive-aggressive sticky note." Listen to their side, even if it's just "I forgot" or "I've had a rough week." Brainstorm fixes—maybe a chore chart, maybe rotating who buys dish soap—then pick something and try it for a while.

When to Seek a Third Party

Sometimes you hit a wall. If the problem escalates—such as unpaid rent, damaged items, or safety concerns—or if talking leads to shouting matches, it's time to call in a third party. In college, Resident Advisors (RAs) are pros at mediating roommate drama and can help everyone find a middle ground. For bigger problems, like unresolved landlord disputes or serious safety issues, you might need to involve someone with real authority. This could be a housing office, tenant union, legal aid clinic, HR representative (for employee housing), or even a trusted neutral friend who doesn't harbor ill feelings toward your roommate. Don't feel weird about asking for help; sometimes, an outsider helps everyone chill out and actually listen.

After any blow-up or awkward chat, don't act like nothing happened. Wait a day or two, then check in: "How's the new cleaning plan working for everyone?" This tiny step prevents resentment from building and allows people to adjust things before the next mess spirals out of control. A little follow-up builds trust and signals that you care about actually getting along, not just winning one argument. Conflict isn't fun, but tackling it head-on makes all your relationships sturdier and way less stressful in the long run.

Understanding Boundaries—How to Set and Respect Them

Boundaries might sound like something you need at a castle, but they're much more useful in daily life—no moat required. In any relationship, you're going to run into all kinds: physical boundaries (like needing space on the couch), emotional boundaries (like not wanting to talk about your ex at breakfast), and digital boundaries (like setting a "no texting after midnight" rule if you're done talking for the day). These lines aren't just for your benefit; they keep things healthy on both sides. Say you want your room to be your sanctuary—maybe you hang a "please knock" sign. Or you're not into sharing every single meme in group chats after 10 p.m. That's a digital boundary.

Bringing up boundaries can feel awkward, especially if you're concerned about sounding harsh or coming across as overly dramatic. But being clear beats letting resentment simmer. Try phrases like, "I need some alone time to recharge after work," or "I'm not comfortable lending out my headphones." If someone asks for your password and you'd rather not share, say, "I'm not comfortable sharing my password, but I can help another way if you need." The trick is using "I" statements—keep things about *your* needs, not their flaws—and let go of guilt. You're not a jerk for having limits. You're just human.

Now, sometimes, you'll be on the receiving end. Maybe a friend says, "Hey, I can't hang out tonight. I really need a mental health day."

Instead of getting salty or defensive, respond with something like, "Thanks for telling me." If you don't understand a boundary, ask about it without grilling them: "Can you help me understand why that's important to you?" Respect goes both ways, and curiosity shows you care about staying connected.

Of course, boundaries are sometimes crossed. Maybe your roommate waltzes into your room without knocking (classic move), or you accidentally post an unflattering photo of your friend. If you cross a line, don't ghost or double down; instead, take responsibility. Admit it: "I'm sorry I walked in without knocking. I'll make sure to check next time." If someone oversteps their boundaries with you, be direct but calm: "I like having privacy in my room—even if the door's open, can you knock first?" If the same boundary keeps getting trampled, it's okay to reinforce it and get specific about what needs to change. Repairing trust takes honesty and sometimes awkward chats, but it beats letting things fester until someone snaps over dirty spoons or borrowed hoodies again. Boundaries are meant to make relationships work better for everyone involved.

Digital Communication—Text, Email, and Social Media Etiquette

If you've ever stared at your phone after seeing "Read 10:06 p.m.," wondering if you've been ghosted or if maybe your friend's distracted, you know the chaos of digital communication. Texting and group chats dominate, but etiquette can be murky. As a general rule, reply within a few hours to close friends and within a day to classmates or acquaintances. No need to answer instantly unless it's urgent ("Pizza or tacos?"). Emojis help set the tone, but don't overdo it—one is enough, and too many, especially odd ones, get you flagged for being weird.

Group chats have their own unwritten rules: Don't spam the chat with unnecessary "LOL"s, and if the conversation turns to making plans, check in with everyone politely—e.g., "Hey all, love you but can't make it this weekend—catch you next time!" That way, you stay clear and polite, and nobody feels left out.

Read receipts are a mixed bag. Some like the openness, while others find it stressful. If they're on, don't leave people waiting too long, or you can expect some passive-aggressive vibes. If you need time, send a "Let me get back to you!" That honesty avoids drama. If you turn read receipts off, that's fine, but don't use it as an excuse to ignore friends.

Email is more formal, primarily when used for school or work purposes, and, unlike texts, clarity and structure matter. Always use a subject line that clearly states the purpose ("Request for Office Hours," not just "Hi"). Greet properly ("Hi Dr. Smith" for professors or "Good morning Alex" for coworkers), then be clear and concise—short paragraphs or bullet points help. Always end with a polite sign-off ("Thanks" or "Best"), your name, and any relevant info (title, class, etc.). When emailing, Reply all only if every recipient truly needs your answer; otherwise, stick to Reply to spare everyone's inboxes.

Social media has even blurrier lines. Your audience might span from best friends to your grandma or future boss. Oversharing (every meal, mood swing, or drama) usually backfires or invites unwanted attention. Before tagging others in posts or photos, always get their permission. Use privacy settings to control who sees your posts; restrict personal updates to close friends or private settings. Consider having separate accounts: one for private memes and casual content, and another for a polished LinkedIn profile for professional networking. On LinkedIn, highlight achievements or skills, not jokes about your weekend.

Digital arguments can become ugly quickly because the tone is often lost. If you feel things heating up in group chats or DMs, pause before replying. Make sure you're not misreading sarcasm or intent, as typed words can be ambiguous. When in doubt, move the conversation offline: "Hey, I think we're misreading each other—can we talk?" This avoids all-caps battles and helps preserve friendships and your sanity.

Reading Social Cues and Handling Awkward Situations

Social cues act like silent subtitles in everyday life; they are often signals that convey more than words. For example, folded arms, averted eyes, or picking up a phone mid-conversation usually mean "I'm done here." Body language reveals a lot: Crossed legs pointing to the exit, fidgeting, or forced laughter all suggest disinterest. If people start checking their phones while you're speaking, you've likely lost their attention. Conversely, nods, eye contact, and leaning in indicate that you have their attention. Recognizing these signals isn't tricky, but it does take practice and awareness. Notice people's posture, their tone, and how quickly they respond. If your joke draws only a courtesy chuckle, it might be wise to change topics.

"Reading the room" is its own kind of superpower. Whether you're at a party, meeting, or new social setting, take a quick mental snapshot before diving in. Are people chatty, or do they seem distant and reserved? Adjust your stories and energy accordingly; perhaps wait to share the wild anecdotes until the mood is lighter. In work meetings, pay attention to who talks the most and who remains silent or appears distracted. If the atmosphere feels tense, tone down on jokes and keep things focused. At family events, test the vibe before sharing potentially controversial or personal details—after all, Aunt Linda might not appreciate your wild dating stories over Thanksgiving dinner. Adjust your volume, humor, and even your language to suit the crowd. Think of it as code-switching: being yourself but adapting your approach so your message lands smoothly.

Even with careful awareness, awkward moments are inevitable. Maybe you call someone the wrong name—for the third time—or overshare at brunch. The best response is a simple, quick apology: "Sorry—I'm terrible with names! Could you remind me?" Or, if you've shared too much, a casual "Wow, that was TMI—moving on!" can lighten the mood and get everyone back on track. The key is not to dwell on the awkwardness or let it ruin the interaction. Everyone slips up. Shrug it off and continue.

What matters most is how you recover from those moments. If you find yourself replaying embarrassing scenes late at night, remember that almost everyone is more concerned with their own slip-ups than yours. Social learning is messy and involves plenty of facepalm moments, but every single one teaches you how to handle things better next time. Give yourself some credit for showing up, trying, and rolling with whatever comes your way. True social confidence comes not from perfection but from embracing a little awkwardness and knowing you can always recover.

Tackling Awkward Work Conversations

Work often feels like a sitcom, except you're the main character, and there's no laugh track when things get awkward. Uncomfortable moments happen more than you'd think—e.g., admitting you messed up a task, explaining why you can't handle more work, or asking your boss for clarification on a cryptic email. Feeling anxious in these moments is normal; work dynamics involve power, unspoken rules, and professional pride. Most people want to appear capable and agreeable, but dodging these talks builds stress.

A plan can help you tackle tricky conversations. When giving feedback, use the "sandwich method": Start with something positive, share the tricky part, and end with encouragement. For example: "I appreciate your quick work on projects. I did notice a couple of details got missed in the last report. Double-checking next time could help. Your effort is valuable here." This way, you're getting your message across and keeping the conversation balanced. If you disagree with a colleague or boss, keep it professional and stick to the idea, not the person: "I see your point, but I have another perspective —can we look at it this way?" This shows respect and avoids conflict.

Gossip and office talk can be tricky. If you overhear inappropriate comments or microaggressions, you can address them without making a scene. Try a quick response like "That's not cool" or "Let's keep it professional," which often resets the conversation. Being left out of meetings or projects can be hurtful, but anger won't help. Instead, approach the organizer and ask, "I noticed I wasn't in the meeting— can you fill me in? I want to stay in the loop." You stay involved without making it personal.

Awkward moments don't have to linger. If you slip up in a meeting or notice tension, follow up with a clarifying email—e.g., "Hey, just wanted to clarify my earlier comments. I value our teamwork." Sometimes, a brief chat in the hallway or over lunch helps restore good vibes: "About earlier—are we good?" Reflecting on what happened and noting how you'd respond differently next time builds confidence for the future. The goal isn't to be perfect but to improve.

Whether trying to understand office dynamics or simply trying to communicate smoothly, remember that everyone feels awkward at times. Each conversation is an opportunity to build trust, rectify missteps, and enhance your ability to handle work's unpredictability.

With these tools, you'll be ready for whatever comes next, including the digital workplace and online safety covered in the following chapter.

Quiz:

1) What is the key difference between active and passive listening?

    A. Active listening includes multitasking; passive listening does not

    B. Active listening focuses on your response; passive listening focuses on silence

    C. Active listening means giving full attention and engaging, while passive listening means hearing without truly understanding

    D. Passive listening is better in emotional situations

Answer: C

Active listening involves full engagement—making eye contact, asking questions, and showing understanding—while passive listening is being physically present but mentally distracted.

2) Which of the following is an example of assertive communication?

    A. "You're always making a mess and it's so annoying."

    B. "Whatever, I'll just do it myself again."

    C. "I feel overwhelmed when the dishes pile up. Can we come up with a plan to keep the space clean?"

    D. Saying nothing and hoping the issue resolves itself

Answer: C

Assertive communication expresses your needs clearly and respectfully, using "I" statements and avoiding blame.

* * *

3) When someone sets a boundary like, "I can't text after 10 p.m.," the best response is:

A. Keep texting until they respond
B. Respect their rule and ask about it if you're curious
C. Call instead, since they didn't say "no calls"
D. Ignore it—it's not a big deal

Answer: B

Respecting boundaries shows maturity. You can also ask politely for clarity without pressuring the other person.

* * *

4) Why is humor considered a powerful tool in clapbacks or handling awkward moments?

A. It avoids addressing the problem
B. It can defuse tension and maintain social balance without escalating conflict
C. It always makes people laugh, even in serious conversations
D. It shows you're tougher than others

Answer: B

Humor, when used thoughtfully, allows you to set boundaries or respond to rude comments without creating more drama.

* * *

5) Which of the following is good digital communication etiquette?

   A. Leaving read receipts on but ignoring messages
   B. Sending group chat replies as one-word texts to stay efficient
   C. Using clear subject lines and greetings in emails
   D. Posting tagged photos without asking

Answer: C

Digital etiquette includes clarity in emails, being respectful in texts, and maintaining boundaries online, like asking before tagging someone.

* * *

Chapter 10

Digital Literacy and Online Safety

Passwords, Privacy, and Protecting Your Digital Identity

Take a moment to relax. You're feeling good, about to start a new semester, and suddenly, your group chat lights up because someone's Instagram got hacked. Suddenly, their account is spamming "weight loss tea" ads, and your inbox is full of weird DMs. It's a joke, until you start worrying if your "password123" is about to betray you. Spoiler: it will.

The truth is, your online life is an extension of your real one. If someone hacks your Snapchat, Gmail, or—worse—your bank login, it's like leaving your apartment door wide open. Weak passwords are the digital equivalent of hiding your key under the doormat. Hackers don't have to try all that hard. What are the most common passwords? Still "123456," "qwerty," and "password." If any of these sound familiar, change them now. And no, "letmein" or your dog's name and birth year aren't clever enough.

So, what makes a strong password you'll actually remember? Try passphrases: unique, memorable sentences with numbers and symbols. For example, "PurpleDuck$Read5Books!" beats "duckie2020." It's long, unforgettable, and much more complicated to guess. Avoid sharing personal information such as birthdays, family or pet names, and sports teams. If you've posted it or put it in your bio, assume someone else can find it.

Password Manager Apps and Two-Factor Authentication

Of course, nobody wants to memorize a hundred passwords. Enter password managers, apps that act as a vault for all your login info behind one master password (which should be a strong passphrase). Free options, such as Bitwarden, and paid ones, such as 1Password or LastPass, are popular. Paid versions offer features such as secure file storage and dark web monitoring, but for most young adults, the free versions are sufficient. To get started, download the app or browser extension from the official site, create your account, and set a master passphrase. Then, let the manager suggest and remind you of strong passwords for new logins. It simplifies everything and boosts your online security.

Now, for two-factor authentication (2FA). This adds a second layer of security to your accounts, so that even if someone has your password, they can't access your account without a code (usually sent to your phone or generated by an app like Google Authenticator or Authy). Most major platforms, including Gmail, Instagram, Facebook, and banks, offer 2FA under the "Security" section in their settings. Please enable it for every important account. It adds a step, but the peace of mind is worth it. Some apps now offer passkey logins using Face ID or fingerprints, eliminating the need for passwords entirely. If your bank or apps support this, go for it. It's quick and secure.

Privacy Settings

Privacy settings are nearly as important as passwords. Social media tends to default to "share everything," so you need to take control of your online presence. On Instagram and Facebook, turn off location sharing for posts and stories unless you want to share your location with strangers. Check who can see your friend list and tagged photos, as the default is often "everyone." Set it to "Friends Only" or "Only Me" if you want more privacy.

Financial apps and info need extra care. Don't use your browser's autofill feature for sensitive information, such as credit card numbers or banking logins. If your device is compromised, your data can easily be stolen. Instead, go into the settings of Chrome, Firefox, or Safari and disable autofill for payment information and passwords on shared or public devices. Use your password manager; if your device is lost, it's less likely to spill your private details.

Oversharing in group chats and DMs is risky, too. Just because it feels private doesn't mean it won't spread. After all, screenshots are forever, and so are your messages venting about work or your landlord. Adjust settings to limit DMs to people you trust, and always think before sending anything sensitive.

Quick Exercise: The Digital Lockdown Challenge

Spend 15 minutes this week on a privacy tune-up as follows:

- **Change the passwords on your three main accounts (email, primary social media, and banking) to strong passphrases.**
- **Download a password manager: Bitwarden (free) or 1Password (for additional features).**
- **Turn on two-factor authentication for at least two major logins.**
- **Set up passkey logins where available.**
- **Review your privacy settings on Instagram and Facebook, and turn off location sharing. Also, consider hiding your friend list and tagged photos.**
- **Disable browser autofill for payment info.**
- **Bonus: Write on a sticky note which accounts now have 2FA or passkey logins and which ones need it next.**

This isn't just busywork; it's building digital armor. With these steps, your online life will be significantly

more secure, providing you with genuine peace of mind.

How to Recognize and Avoid Online Scams and Frauds

Ever gotten a frantic text from "Amazon" about a stuck package or a random email offering a $500 gift card from a bank you don't use? Welcome to the world of online scams. Scammers are persistent and continually adapt their tactics to evade detection. Young adults, in particular, are prime targets. Recognizing their methods is your best protection.

Phishing attacks are common. You'll receive emails or DMs that seem legitimate—claims about a suspended Netflix account or banking issues are typical. Messages lead you to fake login screens that mimic real ones, and if you enter your information, scammers can obtain your credentials. Sometimes, scammers impersonate your college IT or boss, making their requests appear credible, especially when you're distracted or stressed. Real companies won't threaten out of the blue or ask for passwords by email. Look for red flags: typos in addresses (like "amaz0n.com"), bad grammar, and odd formatting.

Fake job offers target students and recent grads. You might receive a message from someone claiming to have found your résumé, offering a remote work opportunity. However, they'll soon ask for your bank information "for direct deposit," send fake checks, request gift card purchases, or attempt to access your Zelle or Venmo account. Any job that pays before you've worked, requires money upfront, or hires without an interview is a scam. Don't share personal info until you research the company and speak with a real person.

Online shopping scams are prevalent, particularly on Instagram, TikTok, and random websites offering huge discounts on sneakers, electronics, or "designer" goods. Sketchy sites might appear polished, but be cautious of missing contact information, suspicious reviews, or prices that seem too good to be true. If you pay, you might get nothing, or your card info could be stolen for fraudulent use elsewhere. Only use secure payment methods, and never send money as "friends and family" to strangers.

Payment app scams are on the rise. Buyers on Facebook Marketplace might ask for Cash App verification via money transfer or say they sent you money by mistake and want it back when, in reality, their original payment was stolen and will bounce. Never share codes sent to your phone, even if someone pretends to be "customer service." Real companies won't ask for codes or passwords outside their secure apps.

Scam Warning Signs

You don't need to be a genius to spot a scam, but you do need to be skeptical. Before clicking links or sending money, check for warning signs: Is the sender's email off or full of random characters? Does the website start with "https"? Hover over links: Does the URL match? If you receive an unexpected attachment, even from a friend, ask before opening it. Scammers sometimes hijack legitimate accounts to spread malware.

Don't trust sites with no contact information or reviews that only appear on their page. Google the company or job title plus "scam" before sharing info or money. Be wary of pressure to act fast, requests for secrecy, or miraculous deals, as they're usually scams. Never download random files from strangers or from friends behaving strangely. Winning a contest you didn't enter is another classic warning sign.

What to Do When You've Fallen for a Scam

If you find yourself caught in the unfortunate event of falling for a scam, you need to remain calm and act promptly. Begin by immediately changing all passwords related to the compromised accounts, ensuring that you log out of these accounts on all devices to prevent further unauthorized access.

In instances where financial information has been disclosed or money has been sent to scammers, your first course of action should be to contact your bank or financial institution. Request that they freeze your cards or accounts to prevent any further unauthorized transactions. For those who have used payment applications such as Venmo or Cash App, it's imperative to reach out to customer support without delay. Many of these platforms offer a grace period within which transactions can be reversed, but immediate action is required.

Should the situation escalate to the point where your Social Security number or other personal information has been compromised, enabling scammers to potentially open new credit accounts in your name, take immediate steps to freeze your credit across all three major credit bureaus—Experian, Equifax, and TransUnion. This preventive measure effectively blocks the opening of new accounts, safeguarding your financial identity.

Furthermore, report the scam to the Federal Trade Commission (FTC) through their official website at reportfraud.ftc.gov. Doing so not only assists in tracking and understanding scam trends but also plays a vital role in helping others avoid falling victim to similar scams. Before deleting any suspicious messages or emails, take screenshots of these communications. They can serve as valuable evidence when reporting the incident to your bank, employer, educational institution, or even law enforcement agencies, should the need arise.

Lastly, it's a good practice to inform your friends and acquaintances if your account has been compromised. This pre-emptive alert can serve as a warning, potentially preventing them from being deceived by scammers who might attempt to exploit your identity to perpetrate further scams.

Scam-Spotter's Checklist

- **Double-check sender addresses for typos and odd characters.**
- **Hover over links before clicking; look for "https."**
- **Google the company, job, or online store with "scam."**
- **Never send money or share codes with strangers or "customer service."**
- **Don't download attachments without confirming with the sender.**
- **If anything feels urgent, stop and check. If it seems too good to be true, it probably is.**
- **If you've been scammed, immediately change your passwords, contact your bank, freeze your credit if necessary, and report to the FTC.**

Online trust should be earned slowly. Pause before trusting anyone new with your info or your money. Scammers bank on you panicking or acting quickly. Stay skeptical and take your time.

Managing Your Online Reputation—What Employers See

Nothing causes anxiety quite like realizing your future boss has found your Instagram. Suddenly, that old meme or cringey video from high school doesn't feel so funny. Our digital footprints linger, even when we outgrow past phases or failed social media stardom. Employers, professors, landlords, and even first dates will look you up online, and what they find can influence real-life opportunities. There are countless tales of graduates losing internships or applicants being ghosted after HR discovers old party photos or off-color jokes. The internet rarely forgets, and sometimes it doesn't forgive.

If that sounds overwhelming, don't worry. Cleaning up your digital presence is totally doable and oddly satisfying. Begin by searching your own name—including nicknames or old usernames—on Google and major platforms. You might discover ancient Tumblr posts or previously tagged photos you had forgotten existed. Don't skip image results. Check platforms such as Facebook, Twitter/X, Instagram, LinkedIn, and TikTok. Review posts, tagged photos, comments, group memberships—anything public. If anything embarrassing appears, delete or untag yourself. Twitter users can utilize apps or built-in features to bulk delete old tweets by date or keyword.

Also, remember your comment history on public groups and pages; even a heated movie debate from 2014 could appear first in search results. Delete or privatize anything you wouldn't want a boss or landlord to see. Tighten your Facebook settings so that only friends can see your posts or your friend list. On Instagram, activate manual review for tags so you can approve them before they show on your profile. For photos outside your control, ask friends to remove themselves from the image or adjust their privacy settings.

If you have old social accounts you never use (hello, MySpace), either delete them or set them to private. The fewer digital skeletons, the better. The goal isn't to erase your personality, just to curate what's public.

Creating Your Online Image

Once you've scrubbed your profiles, actively shape your online image. Rather than letting things happen by chance, share content that reflects your current goals and values. Are you into volunteering? Post photos or stories about causes you support. Want employers to notice your skills? Show off group projects, presentations, artwork, or part-time jobs on LinkedIn. Use a clear profile photo—not overly formal, but avoid blurry group shots or questionable backgrounds.

Think of public profiles as your online billboard: What do you want someone to notice first? Consistency helps; use similar names and images across platforms so it's clear who you are (not a namesake with wild opinions). Especially if you're job hunting or applying for scholarships, check that your bios match your real interests and ambitions.

Celebrate achievements without bragging; support others by sharing their successes. Engage thoughtfully on posts instead of dropping "lol" or sparking arguments. If comfortable, share lessons learned from jobs or activities on LinkedIn. Employers appreciate reflection and growth.

Always respect legal and ethical boundaries. Don't repost someone else's work—art, memes, photos—without permission or credit. Tag creators if you share their content; it's good etiquette and can even help you network. For group photos from events, ask permission before posting publicly; not everyone wants their face online for any reason—job search, privacy concerns, or simply not feeling comfortable.

Remember, copyright applies online as well. Sharing articles, swiping music for videos, or reposting images without rights can get your account flagged or even lead to legal trouble. Use royalty-free music and photos when creating content. If you're sharing borrowed advice, link the source or credit in your post.

Respect privacy on both sides: Avoid publishing screenshots of conversations without consent, even for a laugh. If friends send you something private, don't forward it without checking first. What seems harmless now could resurface unexpectedly later.

Managing your online reputation isn't just damage control; you're being smart by creating chances and avoiding future problems. Treat your digital self as an ongoing project—a little maintenance now saves headaches later and lets you stand out for the right reasons.

Technology for Adulting–Apps and Tools for Smarter Living

If you ever feel like your brain has more tabs open than your browser, you're not alone. When used smartly, technology can clear up the mess, keep your life organized, and save you from the "I forgot to pay rent" panic. There's a digital tool for nearly every adulting headache, and learning how to pick and use them is a huge step toward feeling in control. The trick is to let tech work for you, not run your life (or fry your brain).

Money Apps

Let's start with money. Money apps are basically cheat codes for your budget. Rocket Money (formerly Truebill) is like having an eagle-eyed friend who finds your forgotten subscriptions and gives you a reality check on your spending. If you want a virtual envelope system —where you stash cash in digital "envelopes" for groceries, gas, or entertainment—Goodbudget keeps you honest. For those who want the whole budgeting nerd experience, YNAB (You Need a Budget) will help you plan every dollar and can help you break free from paycheck-to-paycheck living. The point is that you don't have to crunch numbers in your head or keep receipts in random coat pockets anymore. Set up one of these apps, connect your bank, and let them track your spending with way less stress.

Scheduling Apps

Managing your schedule and the avalanche of tasks life throws at you takes more than sticky notes. The Todoist app is a favorite for making lists and setting deadlines, and it syncs across all your devices, so you have no excuses if you "lose" your to-do list. Google Keep is great for quick notes or reminders, especially if you enjoy color-coding everything. Notion offers customizable templates, allowing you to create everything from class planners to mood trackers and packing lists for the trip you keep postponing. Once you set up a system that suits your brain, staying on top of assignments, bills, chores, and goals becomes much more doable. No more "Oops, I forgot" texts are needed.

Health Apps

Health is a big deal once you're on your own and nobody reminds you about doctor appointments or pills. Medisafe sends friendly reminders when it's time to take your medication or vitamins. For mental wellness, Calm and Headspace are two apps that offer guided meditations (some as short as three minutes), breathing exercises, and sleep stories that don't involve counting sheep or existential dread. Even if meditation sounds a little woo-woo to you, taking a minute to breathe can seriously lower stress and make chaos feel less over-whelming.

Let's talk about automation, your future favorite time-saver. Banking apps let you set up recurring bill payments so rent, utilities, or even Netflix get paid automatically on time. No more late fees because a bill vanished into your inbox abyss. For chores or appointments, use calendar apps such as Google Calendar or Apple Calendar to set repeating reminders. Need to water plants every Sunday? Toss it on your calendar once, and never worry about crispy ferns again. Automate reminders for trash day, car maintenance, or even "call grandma" because, let's be real, she deserves it.

But more apps don't equal more freedom. There's a fine line between being tech-savvy and getting buried under digital clutter. If your phone is so packed with apps that it takes three swipes to find Instagram, it's time for a digital spring cleaning. Once a month, scroll through your home screen and delete anything you don't use—yes, even that random language app you downloaded during your "productive quarantine" phase. If you consistently miss emails or lose files in a sea of downloads, that's a sign your digital house needs tidying. Duplicates, old screenshots, endless folders—delete them ruthlessly.

Screen time sneaks up on everyone. Your phone has built-in tracking features (Screen Time on iPhone or Digital Wellbeing on Android) that show you how many hours you spend scrolling through TikTok or doom-scrolling news at 1 a.m. Set app limits if you notice your confidence drops after spending too much time on Instagram or if gaming interferes with your sleep schedule. Tech should make life easier, not distract you into oblivion.

Now, let's talk public Wi-Fi, the sketchy alley of the internet world. Cafes, airports, or libraries tempt you with free Wi-Fi, but logging in to personal accounts on public networks is risky business. Hackers love public hotspots because it's easy for them to snoop on what you're doing or steal passwords if connections aren't secure. Avoid checking bank accounts or sensitive emails on public Wi-Fi unless you use a VPN (virtual private network), which scrambles your data before hackers can grab it. Most browsers show a padlock icon if a site is secure ("https" in the URL); if you don't see it, back away slowly. Always log out of accounts when finished—especially on shared computers.

Tech is supposed to make adulting less painful, not more complicated. Use apps and tools that fit your habits and ditch the rest. Automate what you can so your brain space is freed up for living, not just remembering stuff. And always keep safety in mind when connecting in public spaces.

Tech can handle a lot, but it can't dig your Social Security card out of a messy drawer or magically summon your birth certificate when a new job needs it *today*. That's where the human side of adulting comes into play: You need to know which documents are important, where to find them, and how to keep them secure. Because independence isn't just about digital tools; it's also about being ready when life asks, "Can you prove it?" Next, we'll talk about what you need, why it matters, and how to keep it all organized without turning your room into a filing cabinet.

Quiz:

1) Which of the following is the strongest example of a secure password?

A. 12345678
B. Letmein2020
C. PurpleDuck$Read5Books!
D. MyDogName21

Answer: C

Strong passwords are long, unique passphrases that include symbols, numbers, and upper/lowercase letters—not personal info.

*** * ***

2) What is the main benefit of using two-factor authentication (2FA)?

A. It replaces the need for passwords
B. It guarantees your account can never be hacked
C. It adds an extra layer of security by requiring a second step to log in
D. It makes logging in faster

Answer: C

2FA protects your accounts by requiring a second code (e.g., from your phone), even if someone knows your password.

*** * ***

3) Which of the following is a red flag that suggests an online job offer might be a scam?

A. The company requires a video interview
B. You're asked for bank info or gift card purchases before starting
C. The company has a professional-looking website
D. You receive follow-up emails with a contract

Answer: B

Scammers often ask for money upfront or banking details without a real hiring process—always a red flag.

* * *

4) Why should you regularly review your online presence (e.g., social media, old posts)?

A. To delete old memories
B. So your friends can't tag you anymore
C. To protect your online reputation with potential employers or schools
D. Because platforms delete old content automatically

Answer: C

Employers and others often look up your online presence—cleaning it up ensures they see your best, most professional self.

* * *

5) Which of the following is a smart and safe habit when using public Wi-Fi?

   A. Logging into your bank account
   B. Downloading large files quickly
   C. Using a VPN when accessing private info
   D. Saving all passwords in your browser

Answer: C

VPNs protect your data on public Wi-Fi by encrypting it, making it harder for hackers to steal your information.

* * *

Chapter 11

Planning for the Future

The Essential Documents Checklist: What to Keep and Where

E very independent adult needs a set of documents to function in society. Whether you're opening a bank account, signing a lease, or just trying to get into a bar, the right paperwork matters. The good news is that you don't need a complex filing system; you just need to know what's important and where it lives. Take this as your "adulting passport" checklist.

Start with government-issued identification. You must have at least one piece of photo ID (driver's license, state ID, or passport). They're essential for everything from travel to voting. Your Social Security card? That flimsy piece of paper is vital for jobs, loans, and utilities. Don't carry it daily, but always know where it is and know the number.

Health and insurance cards are next. Always keep your health insurance card in your wallet or phone case for emergencies. The same applies to any prescription, dental, or vision plan cards you might have. Producing the correct card at a doctor's office can save time and stress.

Medical records don't seem necessary—until you switch doctors, need proof for travel or work, or must verify immunizations. Keep copies of your vaccination records, major test results, and any other essential medical documents, including prescriptions for glasses or contact lenses.

Your birth certificate is fundamental; it's proof of your existence. Immigration documents, such as green cards, work permits, or visas (for non-citizens), are just as crucial as they are required for activities such as obtaining a passport, securing employment, and attending school. Never store these in a random drawer.

Financial records are less glamorous but just as necessary: Keep track of your bank account info, student loan paperwork, tax forms (W-2s, 1099s), and pay stubs. These are critical for everything from renting apartments to filing taxes. Choose between keeping paper or digital copies, but keep them sorted and accessible.

Lease or rental agreements (or home-ownership documents) prove your address and legal rights as a tenant or owner. Landlords, banks, or government offices can request these for address verification or disputes.

Keep Track of These Documents

- **Bank account info (routing/account numbers)**
- **Birth certificate (original or certified copy)**
- **Copies of your résumé**
- **Emergency contact list**
- **Employment records (pay stubs, W-2s, offer letters)**
- **Health insurance card**
- **Immigration documents (green cards, work permits, or visas)**

- **Medical records/immunization history**
- **Passport, driver's license, or state ID**
- **Rental lease or housing agreement**
- **Social Security Card**
- **Vehicle registration and insurance**

Now, take a moment and consider the following:

- Do you know where each document is?
- Are any missing?
- Are they safe from fire, flooding, or accidents?
- Could you find them quickly in an emergency?

If you answered "no" or hesitated, you're not alone. Here's how to get organized and protect your documents:

1. First, store original, critical documents (such as birth certificates, Social Security cards, and passports) in a secure yet accessible location. A fireproof or waterproof safe or a sturdy lockbox is best. These are inexpensive and can be tucked away at home, but limit access to yourself and maybe one trusted person.

2. Next: digital backup. Scan or clearly photograph all vital documents and store them in secure, encrypted cloud storage, such as Google Drive, Dropbox, or similar services that support two-factor authentication. Label files for easy retrieval using filenames such as "passport_2025.pdf" or "lease_2024.jpg," instead of something nondescript.

3. Label your physical and digital folders in a way that makes sense for you—e.g., "IDs," "Medical," "Finance," and "Housing." Physical folders can be color-coded; digital folders can be tagged. Ensure it's clear where the most important originals are stored.

4. For your wallet, limit yourself to only the essentials: one photo ID, one health insurance card, one debit or credit card, and perhaps a student ID. Leave items like your Social Security card and original birth certificate at home. Losing any of those with your wallet could lead to serious identity-theft problems, plus they are a pain to replace.

5. Any time your address changes (even just across town), update it promptly on all your official IDs. Most DMVs give you a 30-day window to avoid late fees. Also, update your address with banks, loan providers, insurance companies, voter registration offices, and your landlord to prevent important mail from being sent to the wrong place.

What if something goes missing? Don't panic. For a lost Social Security card, go to the Social Security Administration's website, apply for a replacement, and bring a valid ID. For misplaced passports, especially if they are stolen, report it immediately online or by mail to cancel the old one and initiate the replacement process. Lost driver's licenses require visiting the DMV (many allow you to start the process online). You'll need additional forms of ID and proof of residency, and you'll likely be required to pay a replacement fee.

Sharing Sensitive Documents

Be careful when sharing sensitive documents. Employers may need your Social Security number for tax purposes, but you should never provide it until after an official job offer is made. Landlords sometimes need to verify your ID and income, but never send both sides of your Social Security card by email. Instead, insist on showing originals in person. Schools often request a birth certificate or immunization record for enrollment, but originals should generally be presented in person, not mailed, unless the office explicitly requires it.

If anyone you don't know asks for sensitive documents by unencrypted email ("Just send your passport and SSN as attachments!"), it's a red flag. Respond with: "For security, I can't email these documents. Can I show them in person or use a secure portal?" If someone objects, consider walking away. No job or apartment is worth risking your identity.

Quick ways to decline sketchy requests:

- "I'm happy to provide my documentation at your office, but I won't send it by email."
- "Can we schedule an appointment so I can show the originals in person?"
- "My policy is not to share sensitive info electronically. Is there another way?"

This isn't paranoia; it's common sense. Treat these documents like valuable coins in a video game: hard to replace and crucial for unlocking opportunities. Protecting your information now spares you major headaches later, making life's next steps smoother, whether applying for jobs, signing leases, traveling, or simply proving you exist and are ready for whatever's next.

Yearly Life Audit: Reflect, Reset, and Plan for What's Next

There's something satisfying about hitting reset—not the Wi-Fi router sort, but taking a step back and really reviewing your life. This "life audit" is your chance to pause, reflect on what's working, and ditch what's not before you slide into autopilot. Once a year—maybe New Year's, your birthday, or any time you notice you're just coasting —be your own life coach. No fancy gear is required; find a quiet space, grab some snacks, and get honest with yourself. This is your moment to recognize your wins, call out what's holding you back, and ensure you're not just spinning your wheels.

Start with radical honesty. Think of it as a private confessional in your notes app. What went well this year? Perhaps you chipped away at your debt, made a new friend, or cooked more than just noodles. Celebrate even the small victories. Next, consider what made things tough: Did your budget fall apart fast, were you sick often, or did work swallow your weekends? Write it down, even if it stings. Then check your habits: Are late-night doomscrolling, skipping breakfast, or avoiding chores secretly sabotaging you? Be honest; you can even rate yourself in various areas such as finances, health, relationships, and personal growth.

Divide your audit into big life categories: money, health, relationships, and personal growth. For finances, review how much you spent and saved: Did your coffee habit eat the vacation fund? In health, don't just focus on illness; also consider sleep, diet, and mental well-being. For relationships, cover not just romance but family, group chats, and supportive friends. Personal growth includes hobbies, skills, and whether you tried new things, or just binged another show. This big-picture view shows whether you're balanced or need to shift your focus.

Once you have an honest snapshot, set goals that won't just gather dust. Make them SMART: Specific, Measurable, Achievable, Relevant, and Time-bound. Swap "get healthy" for "walk three times a week" or "save money" for "save $500 by July." These concrete goals let you know what achievement looks like and when it will be achieved. Add deadlines because they make things real. A good SMART goal would be to put $100 a month away for 5 months and save $500 by July 1 to buy a plane ticket to Chicago for your friend's birthday.

Make your goals visible so they don't get lost in daily chaos. Try a vision board with magazine cutouts or a digital Pinterest collage. Tech fans might use Google Keep or Trello for progress tracking. The important part is to keep your goals in mind every day so they stay at the forefront. Set reminders on your phone to give you an extra push when motivation lags.

Small Steps, Big Impact

To bring big dreams to life, break goals into small, manageable steps with timelines. If building an emergency fund is the aim, tasks might include "open a savings account" in January, "set auto-deposit" in February, "skip one takeout meal per week" for the following months, and "review progress" monthly. Link these steps to routines you already have—habit stacking is a powerful approach. Tack a budget review onto another nightly routine, like brushing your teeth, for example. For fitness, tie short walks to breakfast or lunch a couple times a week instead of overhauling your entire lifestyle. Taking small, regular steps makes it easier to maintain and build real momentum.

Milestones and Accountability

Monthly or quarterly check-ins help you stay on track and move forward. Re-evaluate every four weeks: Did you stick to your savings plan? Did those walks actually happen? If not, consider tweaking your approach: Maybe evenings suit you better than mornings. Celebrate milestones early and often: A movie night or a treat for hitting savings targets is more motivating than waiting until the end of the year.

Accountability really matters. Pair up with a friend, sibling, or mentor, someone who will cheer you on and call out excuses. Exchange progress updates over coffee or share a tracking spreadsheet (bonus points for memes). If you prefer solo work, use journaling: Write a "mini–year in review" each month describing what you achieved, what flopped, and how sticking to (or missing) your goals felt. A little reflection keeps you honest and motivated.

Celebrate Progress

Reward your wins, no matter how tiny. Made your bed 30 days straight? Celebrate! Buy that ice cream or crank your favorite playlist. Positive reinforcement works, so treat yourself the way you would encourage a friend.

A yearly audit helps you notice what's most important right now and make adjustments when things change. Some years will be about finances, others about relationships, and sometimes just surviving. If a goal doesn't work out, a side hustle flops, adjust and move on.

Regular check-ins help you spot patterns and gain confidence in making changes before things get out of hand. This process isn't meant to stress you out; it's to give you more control, so adulting feels less like treading water and more like steering your ship, even if the waves get weird sometimes.

End each audit with a lighthearted note—a selfie with your vision board or a meme for your year ahead. Keep these reminders handy for when motivation dips or self-doubt sneaks in. Looking back will prove that, slow though it may be, progress is happening.

Own this process: Pick what works for you, skip what doesn't, and focus on what excites you. Even tiny tweaks can make next year better than the last. This is your reminder: You steer the ship, and every course correction counts.

Building Your Independence Toolbox: Apps and Hotlines

There's nothing like the wild energy of suddenly needing help—your phone screen flickers, you're short on rent, or your mental wellness does that thing where it just... logs off. So you go searching for answers, and the internet throws a thousand links and weird promotional pop-ups your way. The truth is, independence requires more than knowing stuff off the top of your head. You need to know where to look when you need answers fast. That's why building up a personalized "toolbox" of resources, apps, and hotlines is honestly one of the best things you can do for yourself as an adult.

Finance Apps

Start with money, because if adulthood came with a theme song, it'd probably be "Bills, Bills, Bills." Managing finances can feel like juggling flaming torches while riding a skateboard. There's no shame in getting a little digital backup. Budgeting apps like YNAB ("You Need a Budget"), Goodbudget, and EveryDollar allow you to track every dollar, set savings goals, and receive notifications so you don't go overboard on your takeout budget. Rocket Money is another favorite for tracking sneaky subscriptions that drain bank accounts quietly each month.

For actual banking, check your bank's official app; many offer mobile check deposits, spending breakdowns, and bill pay with a few taps. Just make sure to pick an app with a lot of positive reviews and up-to-date security features. No one wants their hard-earned cash vanishing because of a sketchy download.

Health and Wellness Apps

On the health and wellness front, support is just a tap away, even in your pajamas. If you need a quick chat with a doctor or therapist, telehealth platforms like Teladoc or BetterHelp connect you to licensed pros without you ever having to leave your couch. For mental health support, Calm and Headspace offer guided meditations and breathing exercises that can help on anxious days. Medisafe pops up with medication reminders, so you don't have to rely on memory alone. If you're looking for fitness or nutrition ideas, MyFitnessPal and Nike Training Club are packed with routines and meal-tracking features. However, you should double-check their privacy policies before logging every detail of your life.

Career Apps

When it comes to jobs and careers, the right resources can turn desperation scrolling into real progress. LinkedIn is a must—not just for building a shiny profile but for joining groups in your field and connecting with mentors who have been where you are. ResumeGenius and Indeed have free templates to help you create résumés and cover letters that actually get seen by hiring managers. Glassdoor lets you research companies before you apply (or accept an offer), so you know whether that "fun startup" gives vacation time or if it's just code for "work all weekend." Job boards such as Indeed, ZipRecruiter, and Google Jobs are obvious places to start looking for gigs, but don't ignore smaller boards for your city or industry, as they often list opportunities before the big ones catch on.

Legal Help and Crisis-Support Hotlines

Legal help and tenant support might seem intimidating, but certain resources can make the process less daunting. If you ever find yourself stuck in a landlord dispute, tenant rights organizations or legal aid clinics can offer free advice or representation—just Google "[your city] tenant rights" or check out national websites like HUD.gov for housing help. For legal forms or questions that aren't quite "call a lawyer" level but still matter (think: writing a roommate agreement or understanding your lease), sites like Nolo or Rocket Lawyer have plain-English explainers and sample documents.

Crisis moments are when the right hotline can make all the difference. Some numbers are worth saving in your phone even if you hope to never use them. The National Suicide Prevention Lifeline (call 988) is available 24/7 if you or someone you know needs urgent support—real humans will answer, not robots. If texting is more manageable than talking, consider reaching out to Crisis Text Line by texting HOME to 741741. For immediate help with poison emergencies (seriously, if someone drinks cleaning fluid or eats weird mushrooms), call Poison Control at 1-800-222-1222. Domestic violence situations require sensitive help; the National Domestic Violence Hotline at 1-800-799-7233 (SAFE) offers confidential assistance day or night. Housing or food insecurity? Local community resources, such as food banks and housing hotlines, can be found through 211 or by searching "[your city] food bank" online. These organizations exist to help, not judge.

Of course, not all apps and sites deserve your trust. Some financial apps promise to "fix your credit overnight" but are really just after your data—or, worse, your money. Always read reviews in the App Store or Google Play (look for detailed comments, not just star ratings), check for recent updates (an app that hasn't been touched in two years is probably not secure), and do a quick web search for "[app name] scam." Read privacy policies, even if they're boring, to see what info they collect and how they use it. If an app requests unusual permissions (such as access to your contacts or microphone when it doesn't need them), skip it. Watch out for apps with predatory fees—anything that asks for upfront payments or promises guaranteed results should raise red flags. For example, some so-called "financial advisor" apps require huge fees just to tell you what any free blog could share. No, thank you!

Build your own independence toolkit over time. Start simple: Keep a "favorites" folder on your phone with links to your banking app, budgeting tool, telehealth platform, job board, tenant help site, and important hotlines. Bookmark sites you actually use; don't just collect links like digital dust bunnies. During your yearly audit (which you totally do now), review your resources: Are those apps still helpful? Have any gone out of business? Did new needs pop up—like moving to a new city or tackling a new job search? Swap out old links for better ones as life changes.

Staying updated is less about tech wizardry and more about curiosity. Whenever you hit a new life challenge—say, you're suddenly dealing with insurance claims after an accident or realizing your new city has different tenant rules—search for fresh local resources and add them to your collection. Ask friends what they use, too; sometimes, the best tips come from people who have just had the same struggle.

In short, building an independence toolbox means assembling the right combination of digital helpers and real-world contacts so you never feel stuck—or, at least, you know exactly where to look if you do. The best part? This isn't a one-and-done setup; it changes as you do. Whether it's a crisis hotline that gets you through a rough patch or an app that keeps your budget from falling apart after payday, having these tools ready will save time, stress, and sometimes even money.

At this point in your independent life playbook, remember you don't have to do it all alone, and you definitely don't have to memorize everything. With clever use of resources and regular updates to your personal toolkit, you'll be ready for whatever comes next, even if "what comes next" is figuring out how to fix a leaky faucet at midnight or applying for that dream job across the country.

Quiz:

1) Where is the safest place to store original, critical documents like your birth certificate and Social Security card?

   A. Your backpack or wallet
   B. A random drawer in your bedroom
   C. A fireproof/waterproof safe or lockbox at home
   D. Your email inbox

Answer: C

Original documents should be stored securely in a fireproof/waterproof safe or lockbox to protect them from damage and theft.

* * *

2) Which of the following items should you carry with you daily in your wallet or phone case?

A. Social Security card and birth certificate
B. One photo ID, one health insurance card, and one debit/credit card
C. Passport and medical records
D. All your official documents

Answer: B

Carry only what's essential. Leave sensitive documents like your Social Security card and birth certificate at home to reduce identity theft risk.

* * *

3) What is the main purpose of doing a yearly "life audit"?

A. To clean your house
B. To see how many goals you didn't achieve
C. To reflect on what's working, what's not, and to reset your goals with intention
D. To review your Netflix watch history

Answer: C

A life audit helps you evaluate finances, health, relationships, and personal growth so you can make intentional, manageable improvements.

* * *

4) Why is it risky to send sensitive documents like a passport or SSN by regular email?

A. It's inconvenient
B. You might send the wrong file
C. Email can be hacked or intercepted, exposing your identity
D. Employers won't read attachments

Answer: C

Sensitive data sent via unencrypted email is vulnerable. Always use secure methods or show documents in person when possible.

5) What is one benefit of creating a personal "independence toolbox"?

A. You won't need to ask anyone for help again
B. It helps you collect random websites for fun
C. It boosts your social media following
D. It gives you quick access to trusted apps, hotlines, and resources during everyday life or emergencies

Answer: D

An independence toolbox equips you with trusted tools and support systems to handle challenges and stay organized as you navigate adult life.

* * *

Conclusion

Well, you made it. If you're reading this, you're officially at the "did not quit halfway" stage of adulting—which, let's be honest, is a pretty big deal. Take a second and give yourself a high five. Or, if you're in public, maybe just a subtle fist pump. Either way, you've done something incredible: You've taken real steps to build a life that runs on more than ramen noodles and vague hope.

Let's rewind for a minute. When we started this experience, adulting probably felt like some magic trick—one minute, you're a kid; the next minute, you're supposed to know how to fix a leaky faucet, budget for groceries, and talk to people at work without turning into a human question mark. This book wasn't here to hand you the mystical "How to Be a Grown-Up" certificate. Instead, it's your practical, slightly sarcastic toolkit for everyday life.

Remember the big stuff we tackled together? First, we worked on the most important part: your mindset. We ripped the "perfect adult" myth to shreds and replaced it with the truth, that everyone's making it up as they go, and confidence comes from small wins, not overnight genius. You learned how to spot imposter syndrome, set realistic goals, and give yourself credit for progress (even if your biggest win this week was not shrinking your favorite hoodie in the dryer).

Then, we got into the daily grind: time management and organization. No more drowning in to-do lists that look like ancient scrolls. You learned to time-block, use digital calendars, and set up routines that fit your life (and energy levels). Suddenly, getting things done didn't feel like wrestling a calendar that hates you.

Money talk got real. We ditched the stress and confusion by breaking down budgeting, tracking spending, and tackling paychecks and taxes in plain language. You now know how to set up accounts, start an emergency fund, dodge lifestyle creep, and even build credit without falling into a debt pit. Your wallet (and future self) are already sending you thank-you notes.

Hungry for more? You survived the "cooking doesn't have to end in disaster" chapter. You learned which kitchen tools are worth your cash, how to whip up basic (and tasty!) meals, how to prep meals for busy weeks, and how to read nutrition labels without needing a translator. Now, you can feed yourself without relying on "just add water" noodles or the mercy of takeout apps.

Your home is no longer a mystery. We made cleaning, basic repairs, and laundry less intimidating. You've got checklists for daily, weekly, and yearly chores. You know how to unclog a drain, change a light bulb, and handle laundry without accidentally dyeing everything pink. Bonus: You also know your renters' rights and when to call for backup.

But hey, adulting isn't just about stuff and schedules. We also explored health and wellness. Now you know how to book doctor and dental visits, manage stress (existential dread, meet breathing exercises), set up a first aid kit, improve your sleep, and create self-care routines that don't cost a fortune. Your body and mind are officially on your side.

And because being a grown-up means dealing with other humans (which, yes, is sometimes the hardest part), you've picked up practical, real-world communication skills. Active listening, handling awkward conversations, setting boundaries, managing roommate drama—it's all in your toolbox now. You can clap back without drama, resolve conflict without a meltdown, and read social cues like a pro.

Job stuff? You're covered. From résumés and cover letters to networking, interviews, and workplace etiquette, you've got the playbook. You know what to expect during those nerve-racking first days on the job, how to make a decent impression, and how to ask for help without feeling like you've just revealed your deepest secret.

Oh, and let's not forget the digital age. You locked down your passwords, learned to spot scams, managed your online reputation, and picked up the best apps for, well, basically everything. Now, your phone is actually helping you, not just draining your attention span (okay, most of the time).

Here's the thing: You didn't just read a bunch of tips. You built an action plan. You have checklists, step-by-step routines, quizzes, and real-life examples to guide you. Every chapter gave you something you can actually use, whether it's sticking to a budget, meal-prepping for the week, or surviving your first awkward workplace conversation.

If you're feeling a little more confident, a little more independent, and a whole lot less stressed out about how to adult, that's the win. You've already made progress just by learning and trying. Every little step counts.

But let's keep it real: You're not going to get everything right the first time. Keep showing up, practicing, screwing up, laughing (or groaning), and trying again. Keep using the tools in this book. Revisit the quizzes, checklists, and resources whenever life throws something new at you.

And don't be afraid to ask for help. "Community" isn't just a buzz-word; it's a survival tool. Swap stories with friends, share your wins (and fails), and build a support squad that makes the tough stuff easier.

Here's my final nudge: Pick one thing from any chapter—just one. Decide to do it today. Maybe it's setting up a budget, meal-prepping dinner, organizing your documents, or just making that doctor's appointment you've been putting off forever. Momentum comes from action, not from waiting until you "feel ready."

I know you can do this because I started from the same place you are in. I've been the person Googling "how to fix a running toilet" at midnight and texting my mom to ask if it's safe to eat yogurt past the expiration date. I figured it out, and so will you.

So keep this book close. Dog-ear the pages, scribble in the margins, and come back whenever you need a reality check or a pep talk. Adulting is a series of small, brave choices that add up to a confident, independent life. And you? You're well on your way.

Now, go crush it.

References

12 Cooking Skills Every Young Adult Should Learn - Cookist. (n.d.). *Cookist*. https://www.cookist.com/12-cooking-skills-every-young-adult-should-learn/

12 Simple Exercises to Build Confidence In Any Situation. (2024). *The Speaker Lab*. https://thespeakerlab.com/blog/confidence-building-exercises/

14 Netiquette Rules Online Students Should Know. (2024). *University of the Potomac*. https://potomac.edu/netiquette-rules-online-students-should-know/

15 Equally Tasty Substitutes For Beans In Chili - The Rusty Spoon. (2022). *The Rusty Spoon*. https://therustyspoon.com/beans-in-chili-substitutes

21 Ways to Tame Your Tech Budget. (2020). *Consumer Reports*. https://www.consumerreports.org/electronics/technology-telecommunications/ways-to-tame-tech-budget-save-on-bills-a4332979493/

30 Grounding Techniques to Quiet Distressing Thoughts. (2025). *Healthline*. https://www.healthline.com/health/grounding-techniques

The 5 best calendar apps in 2025. (2024). *Zapier*. https://zapier.com/blog/best-calendar-apps/

7 Active Listening Techniques for Better Communication (2024). *Verywell Mind*. https://www.verywellmind.com/what-is-active-listening-3024343

98 Home Repairs You Don't Need to Call a Pro For. (2024). *Family Handyman*. https://www.familyhandyman.com/list/home-repairs-you-can-do-yourself/?srsltid=AfmBOor2YK6tdfJxS-votQJ9WGg5NlQFNMNDifwhUVwneOP-WGKPTsmey

A&B Pro Cleaning. (2023, December 3). *Kitchen cleaning: Tips for keeping the heart of your home*. A&B Pro Cleaning. Retrieved February 23, 2024, from https://web.archive.org/web/20240223100851/https://anbprocleaning.com/3448-whtzoe/

Achieving Financial Strength As A Family In 2024 - Tracy Kiss. (2024). *Tracy Kiss*. https://www.tracykiss.com/lifestyle/achieving-financial-strength-as-a-family-in-2024/

Avoid Lifestyle Creep And Grow Your Savings In 2025. (2025). *Harland Accountants*. https://www.harlandaccountants.com/lifestyle-creep/

Basic Essential Cooking Tools Every Kitchen Needs. (2025). *Cook Smarts*. https://www.cooksmarts.com/cooking-guides/create-a-functional-kitchen/20-must-have-kitchen-tools/

Best Bank Accounts for College Students for May 2025. (2025). *Business Insider*. https://www.businessinsider.com/personal-finance/banking/best-bank-accounts-for-college-students

Best Budgeting Apps of 2025. (2025). *Forbes*. https://www.forbes.com/advisor/banking/best-budgeting-apps/

The Best Password Managers for 2025. (2025). *PCMag.* https://www.pcmag.com/picks/the-best-password-managers

The best subscription trackers of 2025. (2025). *CNBC.* https://www.cnbc.com/select/best-subscription-trackers/

Budget Plans for Young Adults - College Ave. (2024). *College Ave.* https://www.collegeave.com/articles/budget-plans-for-young-adults/

Clean Up Your Digital Footprint: 5 Steps for Job Seekers. (2025). *Heart of the House.* https://www.heartofthehouse.com/clean-up-your-digital-footprint/

Consumer Guide to Tenant and Landlord Rights. (2022). *Office of the Attorney General, Pennsylvania.* https://www.attorneygeneral.gov/wp-content/uploads/2022/06/OAG-Consumer-Guide-Tenant-Landlord-Rights-v.13-web-version.pdf

Developing Your Support System - UB School of Social Work. (2025). *University at Buffalo School of Social Work.* https://socialwork.buffalo.edu/resources/self-care-starter-kit/additional-self-care-resources/developing-your-support-system.html

Discover The Best Dry Seasoning For Broccoli To Elevate Your Dishes To A Whole New - Cookindocs. (2024). *Cookindocs.* https://cookindocs.com/best-dry-seasoning-for-broccoli/

Essential Documents Checklist. (n.d.). *Tennessee Department of Children's Services.* https://www.tn.gov/dcs/program-areas/youth-in-transition/youth-young-adults-resources/essential-documents-checklist.html

First Aid Kits for College & University Students | Red Cross. (2024). *American Red Cross.* https://www.redcross.org/take-a-class/resources/articles/first-aid-kits-for-college-students

Healthy Dinner Recipes for Beginner Cooks. (2020). *EatingWell.* https://www.eatingwell.com/gallery/7577447/healthy-dinner-recipes-for-beginner-cooks/

How to Build Credit With and Without a Credit Card. (2025). *NerdWallet.* https://www.nerdwallet.com/article/finance/how-to-build-credit

How to create the best daily routine: 10 simple habits for .... (2024). *Calm.* https://www.calm.com/blog/daily-routine

How To Do A Life Audit | Ultimate Guide 2024. (2024). *Anam Crae.* https://anam-crae.ca/how-to-do-a-life-audit/

How to Find a New PCP as a Young Adult. (2024). *UPMC.* https://share.upmc.com/2022/06/find-a-primary-care-physician/

How To Make a Resume for Your First Job (With Example). (2025). *Indeed.* https://www.indeed.com/career-advice/resumes-cover-letters/how-to-make-a-resume-for-your-first-job

How to overcome impostor phenomenon. (2021). *American Psychological Association.* https://www.apa.org/monitor/2021/06/cover-impostor-phenomenon

How to read a pay stub. (2022). *Consumer Financial Protection Bureau.* https://files.consumerfinance.gov/f/documents/cfpb_building_block_activities_how-to-read-pay-stub_handout.pdf

How to Report a Passport Lost or Stolen. (2025). *U.S. Department of State.* https://travel.state.gov/content/travel/en/passports/have-passport/lost-stolen.html

How To Season Frozen Vegetables - Jooever. (2023). *Jooever.* https://www.jooever.com/news/how-to-season-frozen-vegetables.html

How to Understand and Use the Nutrition Facts Label. (2024). *U.S. Food & Drug Administration.* https://www.fda.gov/food/nutrition-facts-label/how-understand-and-use-nutrition-facts-label

How To Use the STAR Interview Response Technique. (2025). *Indeed.* https://www.indeed.com/career-advice/interviewing/how-to-use-the-star-interview-response-technique

How to: become a better cook | easyFood. (2018). *easyFood.* https://easyfood.ie/kitchen_tips/become-a-better-cook/

Laundry Basics | The American Cleaning Institute (ACI). (2025). *American Cleaning Institute.* https://www.cleaninginstitute.org/cleaning-tips/clothes/laundry-basics

Meal Prep 101: A Beginner's Guide to Meal Prepping. (2018). *Budget Bytes.* https://www.budgetbytes.com/meal-prep-101-a-beginners-guide/

Mindsets and Perfectionism - by Brian McCormick. (2025). *Substack.* https://brianmccormick.substack.com/p/mindsets-and-perfectionism

Securing your Instagram account with two-factor .... (2025). *Instagram.* https://help.instagram.com/566810106808145

Setting Healthy Boundaries in Relationships. (2025). *HelpGuide.* https://www.helpguide.org/relationships/social-connection/setting-healthy-boundaries-in-relationships

Sleep hygiene: Simple practices for better rest. (2025). *Harvard Health Publishing.* https://www.health.harvard.edu/staying-healthy/sleep-hygiene-simple-practices-for-better-rest

Student's Guide to LinkedIn. (n.d.). *LinkedIn.* https://careers.linkedin.com/content/dam/me/careers/StudentCareers/about/LI-Students-Guide-To-LinkedIn.pdf

Time Blocking - Your Complete Guide to More Focused Work. (2025). *Todoist.* https://www.todoist.com/productivity-methods/time-blocking

Top 4 scams that target young adults - DFPI - CA.gov. (2025). *California Department of Financial Protection and Innovation.* https://dfpi.ca.gov/news/insights/top-4-scams-that-target-young-adults/

Top Email Etiquette Examples for Professional .... (2025). *Indeed.* https://www.indeed.com/career-advice/career-development/email-etiquette-examples

The Ultimate Home Maintenance Checklist for Every Season. (2024). *Better Homes & Gardens.* https://www.bhg.com/home-improvement/advice/home-maintenance-checklist/

Why Students Should Use the Eisenhower Matrix (With ...). (2025). *Productivity Patrol.* https://productivitypatrol.com/eisenhower-matrix-for-students/

Yale University. (2025). *Using DESC to make your difficult conversations more effective* [PDF]. Yale University. https://your.yale.edu/sites/default/files/2025-03/adviformanagers_usingdesctomakeyourdifficultconversations.pdf

Bonus - Downloadable
Budget Spreadsheets

Use this link for budget spreadsheets if you have a Google account and want to save the file to your Google Drive:

Use this link for budget spreadsheets if you have Microsoft Excel:

www.ingramcontent.com/pod-product-compliance
Lightning Source LLC
Chambersburg PA
CBHW051621120626
46551CB00014B/1893